WORDS OF ENLIGHTENMENT
FROM THE DALAI LAMA

COMPASSION

"Compassion compels us to reach out to all living beings, including our so-called enemies, those people who upset or hurt us. Irrespective of what they do to you, if you remember that all beings like you are only trying to be happy, you will find it much easier to develop compassion towards them."

FREEDOM

"As this dramatic century draws to a close, it is clear that the renewed yearning for freedom and democracy sweeping the globe provides an unprecedented opportunity for building a better world. Freedom is the real source of human happiness and creativity. Only when it is allowed to flourish can a genuinely stable international climate exist."

HUMAN RIGHTS

"Discrimination against persons of a different race, against women, and against weaker sections of society may be traditional in some places, but because they are inconsistent with universally recognized human rights, these forms of behavior should change. The universal principle of the equality of all human beings must take precedence."

THE
DALAI LAMA'S
BOOK OF
WISDOM

Edited by

Matthew E. Bunson

RIDER
LONDON • SYDNEY • AUCKLAND • JOHANNESBURG

7 9 10 8

Copyright © Matthew E. Bunson, 1997

Matthew E. Bunson has asserted his moral right to be identified as the author of this work in accordance with the Copyright, Design and Patents Act 1988.

All rights reserved. No part of this publication may be reproduced, stored in a retrieval system, or transmitted in any form or by any means, electronic, mechanical, photocopying or otherwise, without the prior permission of the copyright owner.

First published in 1997 by Plume, an imprint of Dutton Signet, a member of Penguin Putnam Inc., USA

This edition published in 1998 by Rider, an imprint of
Ebury Press
Random House UK Ltd
Random House
20 Vauxhall Bridge Road
London SW1V 2SA

Random House Australia (Pty) Ltd
20 Alfred Street
Milsons Point Sydney
New South Wales 2016 Australia

Random House New Zealand Limited
18 Poland Road, Glenfield
Auckland 10 New Zealand

Random House South Africa (Pty) Limited
Endulini, 5A Jubilee Road
Parktown 2193, South Africa

Random House UK Limited Reg. No. 954009

Papers used by Rider Books are natural,recyclable products made from wood grown in sustainable forests.

Printed and bound in Great Britain by Mackays of Chatham, plc

A CIP catalogue record for this book is available from the British Library

ISBN 0 7126 7119 6

This book is dedicated, with the deepest respect, to His Holiness the XIV Dalai Lama of Tibet and to the courageous people of Tibet

Acknowledgments

There are many individuals to whom a special debt of thanks is owed for their invaluable assistance in the preparation of this work. First and foremost, I would like to thank His Excellency Dawa Tsering, representative of His Holiness the XIV Dalai Lama to North America. Without his kindness and the cooperation of the Tibetan government-in-exile this book would not have been possible. Thanks are also owed to Glen Kelley, special assistant to Dawa Tsering; the staffs of several libraries, including the Sahara West Library; Elke Villa; Marylou Hale; Kim Clanton-Green; Marie Cuglietta; Jane Cavolina; Deirdre Mullane; Eben Weiss; Martha Casselman, my exceedingly patient agent; Margaret and Stephen Bunson; and especially Danielle Perez, my editor at Dutton, for her confidence, enthusiasm, and friendship.

Contents

PART ONE

THE LIFE OF TENZIN GYATSO, THE XIV DALAI LAMA OF TIBET

PART TWO

THE WISDOM TEACHINGS OF THE DALAI LAMA

Section One
Dharma and Religion

Section Two
The World and Tibet

P A R T   T H R E E

THE OCCUPATION OF TIBET   229

Appendices

Introduction

Tibetans and believers who accept His Holiness Tenzin Gyatso the XIV Dalai Lama of Tibet as the living incarnation of *Avalokiteshvara* (or *Chenresig* in the Tibetan), the Buddha of Compassion, use a special honorific title in describing their beloved teacher: *Kundun*. Meaning the Presence in Tibetan, *Kundun* denotes the spiritual power and eminence of the Dalai Lama, and it has an undeniable significance for all who have listened to his discourses, have attended a ceremony over which he has presided, or simply have observed him in the company of his monks, nuns, and eager students.

Dressed in his saffron-and-maroon-colored robes, speaking in an often broken English, and peering at the world through eyes that have lost none of their wonder and decency despite the horrors he has witnessed, the Dalai Lama is seemingly out of place in the modern world. And yet, the religious leader commands the attention of the world by utilizing its most advanced methods of communication and travel. He journeys on jet aircraft, writes books and articles, speaks on television, and has even encouraged his embassies (the Offices of Tibet) to have their own sites on the World Wide Web. All of these efforts, however, are mere tools to aid the Dalai Lama in posing to all whom he meets the same challenge: to join a quest for inner peace and spiritual attainment that defies the ephemeral modern age and focuses the heart and mind on what is real and eternal. This challenge is one taken up willingly and with the full acknowledgment of his supporters that his words are of benefit to their lives and that his cause for Tibetan freedom truly is a just one.

This presence and the immense value of his teachings have made him, with Mahatma Gandhi, Mother Teresa of Calcutta, and Pope John Paul II, one of the genuinely transcendent spiritual figures of the twentieth century. Like these three remarkable teachers, the Dalai Lama has been able to reach beyond his Buddhist devotees to find a universal relevance. He has followers from among the Catholic, Jewish, Muslim, agnostic, and even atheist communities. Those who revere him do not necessarily adopt Buddhist practices, but virtually all derive spiritual and mental enrichment from his insights on daily living, inner peace, compassion, peace and justice, and the environment.

This self-proclaimed "simple Buddhist monk's" qualifications to speak about such matters are unimpeachable. The exiled leader has seen all the myriad dangers facing the modern world unleashed upon his own country: war, ecological destruction, and the trampling of human rights, political justice, and religious freedoms in the name of supposed political, economic, and ideological progress. It is this firsthand experience with the many faces of suffering that makes him so authentic a teacher, and it is the profound depth of his belief that has permitted him the patience and the compassion to forgive his enemies, to be ceaseless in his optimism for peace, and to bear upon himself the anguish of the Tibetan people.

The Wisdom Teachings of the Dalai Lama is intended to provide a collection of the lessons and insights of this exiled religious leader. While grounded in the richest traditions of Tibetan Buddhism, this compilation is for all who wish to study the unique, timely, and often startling perspectives of the Dalai Lama on the challenges facing the human heart, including peace, love, religion, compassion, justice, and the modern world, as well as his views on the three subjects of greatest concern to him: the preservation of the environment, the liberation of Tibet, and the bringing of Buddhism to the awareness of the West.

For those readers who are not familiar with the life of the Dalai Lama, a good place to start would be reading his brief biography in Part One, including his discovery as the reincarnation of the XIII Dalai Lama and the seizure of Tibet by the People's Republic of China, which forced him to flee to India in 1959. It might then be useful to turn to Part Three, which presents an overview of Tibetan history, focusing on the occupation of the kingdom by China and the current state of affairs in Tibet, the Land of the Snows. These sections tell briefly of Tibet's torment, why the Dalai Lama has traveled, written, and spoken so tirelessly to bring about the release of his nation from its long captivity, and how it is that the Dalai Lama has come to be described by so many, including American Congressman Mel Levine, as "a symbol of peace and a leading international spokesperson for the cause of nonviolent social change."

Those who wrong me, and those who accuse me
falsely, and those who mock me, and others:
May they all be sharers in Enlightenment. I
would be a protector for those without
protection, a leader for those who journey, and
a boat, a bridge, a passage for those desiring the
farther shore.
For all creatures, I would be a lantern for those
desiring a lantern, I would be a bed for
those desiring a bed, I would be a slave
for those desiring a slave.
I would be for creatures a magical jewel, an
inexhaustible jar, a powerful spell, a universal
remedy, a wishing tree, and a cow of plenty.
As the earth and other elements are, in various
ways, for the enjoyment of innumerable beings
dwelling in all of space,
So I may be in various ways, the means of
sustenance for the living beings occupying
space, for as long a time as all are not satisfied.

—**From Santideva,**
*Entering the Path of
Enlightenment (Bodhicaryavatara)*

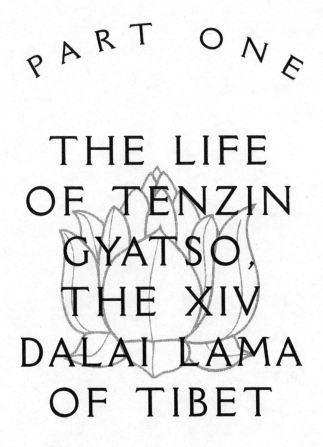

PART ONE

THE LIFE OF TENZIN GYATSO, THE XIV DALAI LAMA OF TIBET

I am a simple
Buddhist monk,
no more, no less.

In 1933 the XIII Dalai Lama of Tibet, Tupden Gyatso, died after a reign as spiritual and temporal leader of the Tibetan people of over a half century. His passing cut short his highly anticipated program of reform for the Kingdom on the Roof of the World which might have done much to bring the isolated land into the twentieth century. The beloved Dalai Lama had stressed the urgency of reforming the political, social, and economic structures of Tibet, prophesying just before his death that the Land of the Snows—as the Tibetans term their own mountainous realm—was in danger of being overrun, its people slaughtered, and its sacred beliefs crushed beneath an enemy's terrible might. The prophecy was made all the more chilling by the recognition by Tibetan leaders that to the east there was rising a shadow of danger from China, which had harbored ambitions for centuries of adding Tibet to its vast territorial possessions.

It was thus in an atmosphere of deep trepidation for the future that the search commenced to find the successor to Tupden Gyatso. For Tibetans this quest meant far more than finding the political ruler of the ancient feudal

kingdom. The Dalai Lama was, for them, the physical reincarnation of the Buddha of Compassion, Chenrezig
(Avalokiteshvara in the Indian), a Bodhisattva (or Enlightened Being) who has made the decision out of love
and compassion for all humanity to decline Nirvana, salvation itself, and return to the world to aid others on their
path to Enlightenment. Knowing the difficult tasks which
were to be faced by the new Dalai Lama and the incompa-
rable importance of the Lama to the Tibetan people, the
governmental and religious officials who gathered in
Lhasa chose carefully the Regent, the leader in charge of
finding the reincarnation. The lama they chose was Reting Rinpoche.

The Regent had only a few precious clues on which to
base his search. As death approached the XIII Dalai Lama,
Tupden Gyatso had predicted that his rebirth might come
in the eastern part of Tibet. After his death several portents seemed to corroborate this possibility. Clouds and
rainbows pointed eastward; a fungus grew inexplicably
on the eastern part of a pillar in the Potala Palace, the
sacred residence of the Dalai Lamas in Lhasa; and, though
the dead lama's head had been pointed to the south, attendants discovered that it had turned toward the east.

With these omens in his mind, Reting Rinpoche took a
trip to the holy lake of Lhamo Lhatso, a place well known
for imparting visions upon its visitors. The Regent beheld
there a vision of a monastery with a roof of jade green
and gold, a house with turquoise tiles, and a yard with a
brown and white dog. Reting also beheld three Tibetan
letters, *Ah*, *Ka*, and *Ma*, although their meaning was un-
clear. Reting returned at once to Lhasa and, divulging the

secret revelations to a select group of lamas, he sent them out in search parties across Tibet.

One of the search parties, under the direction of the trusted lama Kewtsang Rinpoche of Sera Monastery, set out for the eastern part of the country. Reaching the rugged and distant province of Amdo in the northeast in 1937, the searchers came to the village of Takster and there found a monastery with a roof of jade and gold. Exploring the village, they came upon a house with turquoise tiles. Within was a family with a two-year-old boy. He was named Lhamo Dondrub.

Disguised as a servant and with the junior official Lobsong Tsewang pretending to be the chief of the party, the now anxious Kewtsang Rinpoche spoke to the child and was surprised to hear him demand the rosary Kewtsang was wearing; the rosary had once belonged to the XIII Dalai Lama. Kewtsang promised to give the rosary to the boy if he could guess who he was and give the correct name of the party's leader. The boy replied that Kewtsang was *Sera aga*, a colloquial way of saying a "lama of Sera." He then correctly identified Kewtsang by name, gave the name of Lobsong Tsewang, and declared matter-of-factly that Kewtsang was leader of the party. The importance of the letters was now suddenly clear to Kewtsang. *Ah* meant Amdo Province, *Ka* stood for Kumbune (the largest monastery in the area), and *Ka* and *Ma* denoted Karma Rolpai Dorji (the monastery with the roof of jade and gold).

Kewtsang soon met with the child alone and performed a series of exacting tests and examinations. Lhamo passed each of them, and the lama noted that he also bore the traditional marks of the reincarnated Dalai Lamas: large ears, long eyes, and a conch-shell birthmark upon the hand. Finally, state oracles were consulted. They confirmed the joyous news that the reincarnation of the XIII Dalai Lama had been found.

Preparations were made to bring the child to Lhasa, but, in a foreshadowing of the shattering events to come in the life of the new Dalai Lama, a local Chinese warlord, Ma Bufeng, demanded an enormous sum of money from the Tibetans before allowing the sacred child to leave his region. The ransom was paid with difficulty, and the procession set out, reaching Lhasa on October 6, 1939. Two days later, to the musical accompaniment of "God Save the King" and the wild cheers of the crowds, the new Dalai Lama was brought into Lhasa. Several weeks later, Lhamo Dondrub was ordained a Buddhist monk, receiving the new name Jetsun Jamphel Ngawang Losang Yeshe Tenzin Gyatso, meaning the Most Venerable, Elegant, Glory, Eloquent, Intelligent, Defender of the Faith, Ocean of Wisdom. Finally, on February 22, 1940, the newly named Tenzin Gyatso was enthroned officially as the XIV Dalai Lama.

The Dalai Lama spent the next years in deep study of Buddhism. Government remained in the hands of regents until the assumption of full authority by the Dalai Lama in November 1950. The impetus for this dramatic step—he was barely sixteen at the time—was the rise of the People's Republic of China, which claimed control of China following World War II. The communist regime made clear its intention of seizing Tibet.

Omens and grim portents were seen anew in Lhasa.

An earthquake struck the area, a comet crossed a blood red sky in late 1949, and the top of one of the Potala's most ancient columns was found broken. The significance of the column was not lost on state oracles. It had been erected to commemorate a victory over China in 763. The oracles conducted their divinations and insisted that the Dalai Lama assume full control of the state.

Such a step came only just in time. The Chinese People's Liberation Army rolled across the frontier in October 1950 and gained a foothold in the country. Less than a year later, on September 9, 1951, Chinese troops marched into Lhasa. Within months there were over twenty thousand Chinese troops stationed in Lhasa alone. The nation was at the mercy of its new overlords.

Accepting the reality of the situation, the Dalai Lama entered into negotiations with the Chinese, even accepting an invitation to visit Beijing to confer with Mao Zedong. By the time of his return home, however, the Chinese were well advanced in their plans for the collectivization of property and stamping out the religious faith of the Tibetans, which they saw as backward and antithetical to the spread of communism. The Tibetans resisted the oppression, and China responded with brutal crackdowns, arrests, and imprisonments.

While negotiating with China and trying to hold his people together, the Dalai Lama continued his comprehensive Buddhist education. Having started at the age of six to master and live the Dharma (the teaching of the Buddha), he spent long years in study with the finest monks and teachers in the kingdom at the respected universities of Sera, Drepung, and Ganden. At the age of twenty-four he completed the first set of grueling examinations, culminating the next year (1959) with the attainment of a doctorate in Buddhist philosophy, the *Geshe Lharampa*. He wrote of his experience in *My Land and My People* (1964):

> In the morning I was examined on Pramana, or logic, by thirty scholars turn by turn. . . . In the afternoon fifteen scholars took part as my opponents in debate. . . . In the evening there were thirty-five scholars to test my knowledge of Vinaya, the canon of monastic discipline, and Abhidharma, the study of metaphysics. And at each session hundreds of learned lamas in their brilliant red and yellow robes—my own tutors anxiously among them—and thousands of monks sat around us on the ground, eagerly and critically listening.

In the midst of the preparations for the final examinations and as the political situation in Tibet deteriorated daily, a message was delivered by the local Chinese general that the Dalai Lama should join him at a theatrical performance in the Chinese military compound in Lhasa. The message stipulated further that he was to come alone. This demand was greeted with considerable alarm by the court. Chinese efforts to shatter the love of the people for the Dalai Lama and to loosen the hold of Buddhism upon the Tibetan culture had proven futile, and tensions were rising from fear that Beijing might take some drastic actions such as kidnapping the Dalai Lama. Thus, what began as a private invitation soon caused widespread upheaval in Lhasa when Beijing Radio announced publicly that the Dalai Lama would attend the performance.

Even as court ministers plotted ways for the Lama to escape Tibet, the Tibetans took to the streets in a mass protest at dawn on March 10, 1959. The event signaled what came to be called the National Uprising, and the Dalai Lama, within his summer palace of the Norbulingka, sat in immense sadness at the direction events were taking. He wrote: "I could not approve of violence, and so I could not approve of the violent attitude the people of Lhasa were showing. I could and do appreciate the affection for me, as the symbol of Tibet, an attitude which was the immediate cause of the anger they were showing against the Chinese on that fateful day.

Claiming that they wished to "free" the Dalai Lama from a "reactionary clique," the Chinese troops opened fire with mortars on the crowds outside the Norbulingka. Relations with China were in tatters, and the Dalai Lama was left with only one option. He must flee the country:

> A soldier's clothes and a fur cap had been left for me, and about half past nine I took off my monk's habit and put them on. And then in that unfamiliar dress, I went to my prayer room for the last time. I sat down on my usual throne and opened the book of Lord Buddha's teachings which lay before it, and I read to myself till I came to a passage in which Lord Buddha told a disciple to be of good courage. Then I closed the book and blessed the room, and turned down the lights. As I went out, my mind was drained of all emotion. I was aware of my own

sharp footfalls on the floor of the beaten earth, and
the ticking of the clock in the silence.

He took off his glasses to further the disguise and
walked out the gate of the Norbulingka Palace "unchal-
lenged toward the dark road beyond." That road took
him to the Himalayas and the dangerous trek down into
India. As he journeyed with his closest companions,
Beijing declared the Tibetan government dissolved and
launched a merciless campaign of retribution upon the
Tibetan people. With the enormous task of establishing a
government in exile, finding some means to help his
stricken people, and organizing international help, the
Dalai Lama reached Dharamsala, India. He has never returned to Tibet.

The flight of the Dalai Lama signaled the escape of tens
of thousands of Tibetans into India and Nepal. Most who
survived the trip—many died in the mountains or were
shot on sight by Chinese troops for trying to leave the
country—found themselves in refugee camps where the
principal means of surviving was to accept work digging
roads and building other camps for the constant flow of
refugees. Working with the government of India, the
Dalai Lama and his ministers tried to improve conditions
and to prepare for what he knew would be a long and
painful exile. Beyond the supplies of food and medicine, a
serious concern was to make arrangements for the preservation of Tibetan culture under the dire circumstances
of the Tibetan occupation and the separation of so many
Tibetans from their homeland.

Nestled at the base of the Himalayas in the Kangra district of the Indian state of Himachal Pradesh, Dharamsala became the center for the Tibetan government-in-exile and soon acquired the nickname "Little Lhasa." The Dalai Lama established offices for government administration, libraries to house the texts smuggled out of Tibet, and schools. Tibetan leaders next struggled to create self-sustaining communities out of the far-flung refugee camps in India, Nepal, Bhutan, and in the West. Through patience and diligence, the camps became successful communities, and the Tibetans proved to be hardworking and adroit businesspeople who maintained excellent relations with their Indian hosts.

Coinciding with the rebuilding of Tibetan society in exile was the effort to reconstruct Tibetan monasticism, which had been for centuries a pillar of life in Tibet. The Dalai Lama reestablished the great monasteries of Drebung, Sera, Ganden, and Namgyal (the personal monastic institution of the Dalai Lama), which began training novices and bestowing degrees in Buddhism. There are currently more than two hundred reconstituted monasteries and convents. With these and other institutions devoted to preserving and promoting Tibetan culture: Tibet House, the Library of Tibetan Works and Archives, the Tibetan Institute of Performing Arts, the Central Institute for Higher Tibetan Studies, the Tibetan Medical and Astrological Institute, and the Center for Tibetan Arts and Crafts.

Politically, the Dalai Lama focused on two main objectives. First, there was the ongoing process of reform and democratization for the Tibetan people. Second was the effort to galvanize international support for his nation's cause.

The aspiration of the XIII Dalai Lama for genuine reform in Tibet was one of the legacies bequeathed to his successor. The stated hopes of the XIV Dalai Lama to bring about this meaningful social and political betterment were never realized, owing to the pace of events which overwhelmed Tibet. The chief obstacle, of course, was the Chinese occupation and the seizure and collectivization of all Tibetan property. Once in Dharamsala, however, the Dalai Lama moved quickly to fulfill his dreams. In 1963 he promulgated a democratic draft constitution for a Free Tibet, an act which served as the basis for subsequent changes.

The Tibetan government-in-exile was arranged into three branches, the executive (called the Kashag, or Council of Ministers), legislative (the Assembly of Tibetan People's Deputies, ATPD), and the judicial (the Tibetan Supreme Justice Commission). Each branch has contributed to reforms and modernization, but the pace of change has been spurred forward by the Dalai Lama, who willingly surrendered his feudal rights over the Tibetans and took two significant steps in recent years to advance democratization. In 1990 he dissolved the Tenth Assembly and the Kashag, which had been appointed by him, and insisted upon new elections. For the election of the Eleventh Assembly (which then chose the members of the Kashag), the Dalai Lama called for a one-person, one-vote system. The forty-six members were chosen by free elections with ten members coming from the three provinces traditional to Tibet (Amdo, Kham, and U-Tsang), two from each of the four schools of Tibetan Buddhism (Nyingma, Sakya, Kagyu, and Gelukpa) and Bon (the indigenous shamanistic religion of Tibet); three members were nominated by the Dalai Lama; and in a remarkable innovation, three members were chosen from outside the customary provinces of Tibet or the religious bodies. Two of the members represented Tibetan interests in Europe while the third spoke for those exiled in America. The Assembly was then empowered to elect the members of the Kashag, filling such ministries as Finance, Health, International Relations, and Education.

After the success of the elections, the Dalai Lama completed his reforms by issuing a policy statement in 1992 guaranteeing that when Tibet regains its independence, he will make no claim to his historical and political authority and will live as a private citizen. Further, by the terms of the Charter for Tibetans in Exile, Tibet will be a free and democratic state after independence with guarantees of freedom of speech, belief, and movement.

From the earliest time of his exile, the Dalai Lama attempted to bring about a peaceful, negotiated settlement with China that would permit his return to Tibet and secure either autonomy or independence for the Tibetans. While the Lama failed to stimulate international support in 1956 during his trip to India, the bloody events of 1959 and his astonishing escape over the Himalayas captured the attention of the world. Soon after his arrival in Dharamsala, the United Nations passed the first of three resolutions (the other two were in 1961 and 1965) expressing concern over the human rights situation in Tibet and calling for "the cessation of practices which deprive the Tibetan people of their fundamental human rights and freedoms, including the right to self-determination."

Building on the growing international support for his country and to begin visiting Tibetans in exile across the globe, the Dalai Lama made his first visit to the West in 1973, touring Europe and meeting with Pope Paul VI in the Vatican. From that initial sojourn began the Lama's many travels, which have taken him to forty-six countries, including Israel, Mexico, South Africa, Russia, Canada, and Argentina. He has been the guest of Queen Elizabeth II, Pope John Paul II, and numerous presidents and heads of state. In 1991 he became the first foreigner to address the Parliament of the recently freed country of Lithuania. He first visited the United States in 1979 and now makes an annual trip to Washington, D.C., to meet with American leaders and the members of the sizable Pro-Tibetan community. His trip to America was the cause of much excitement to Tibetans, for it seemed to fulfill a prophecy made in the eighteenth century by Padmasambhava:

When the iron bird flies and horses run wheels, the Tibetan people will be scattered like ants across the face of the earth, and the dharma will come to the land of the red men.

While traveling, the Dalai Lama has continued to plead for international help for Tibet and to ask China to negotiate a settlement. To advance the process of reconciliation, he took the dramatic step of offering a Five-Point Peace Plan, delivered at the United States Congress's Human Rights Caucus on September 21, 1987. He declared:

I wish today to clarify the principal issues and to propose, in a spirit of openness and conciliation, a first step toward a lasting solution. I hope this may contribute to a future of friendship and cooperation with all of our neighbors, including the Chinese people.

This peace plan contains five basic components:

1. Transformation of the whole of Tibet into a zone of peace

2. Abandonment of China's population-transfer policy, which threatens the very existence of the Tibetans as a people

3. Respect for the Tibetan people's fundamental human rights and democratic freedoms

4. Restoration and protection of Tibet's natural environment and the abandonment of China's use of Tibet for the production of nuclear weapons and dumping of nuclear waste

5. Commencement of earnest negotiations on the future status of Tibet and of relations between the Tibetan and Chinese peoples

Claiming that the plan was intended only to widen the gulf between China and the Tibetan government-in-exile, Beijing rejected the Dalai Lama's offer outright. Later that year a fourteen-point note was sent to the Chinese government elucidating the plan. Even further elaboration was made by the Dalai Lama on June 15, 1988, at the

European Parliament at Strasbourg, focusing on the final point, negotiations on the future status of Tibet. These appeals were again met with a cool reception by China, but the Dalai Lama's continued efforts earned him widespread acclaim and was a decisive factor in his being honored with the 1989 Nobel peace prize. The committee declared in its citation:

> The committee wants to emphasize the fact that the Dalai Lama in his struggle for the liberation of Tibet consistently has opposed the use of violence. He has instead advocated peaceful solutions based upon tolerance and mutual respect in order to preserve the historical and cultural heritage of his people.
>
> The Dalai Lama has developed his philosophy of peace from a great reverence for all things living and upon the concept of universal responsibility embracing all mankind as well as nature.
>
> In the opinion of the committee the Dalai Lama has come forward with constructive and forward-looking proposals for the solution of international conflicts, human rights issues, and global environmental problems.

China responded by denouncing the committee for its "interference in internal Chinese affairs." Beijing subsequently rejected all efforts to begin negotiations, placing insurmountable obstacles in the way or insisting upon preconditions to talks which would have rendered the final objective of a settlement to the Tibetan question unobtainable. Beijing also refused to permit representatives of the Dalai Lama to assist—as is their right—in finding the reincarnation of the late Panchen Lama.

Still committed to negotiations in what he termed the "Middle Way," the Dalai Lama made yet two more overtures. First, in an address at Yale University in October 1991, he requested that he be permitted to see for himself the conditions in his homeland. Second, two months later, he asked to meet with Chinese prime minister Li Peng during the Chinese official's visit to India. Both appeals were rebuffed.

Acknowledging the futility of further petitions, the Assembly of Tibetan Deputies passed a resolution on January 23, 1992, stating the Tibetan government's position that no new initiatives would be made until China itself adopted a new attitude. The Tibetans, however, would welcome any initiative from the People's Republic of China. Despite these frustrations the Dalai Lama remains optimistic and has said on many occasions that he is ready to meet with Chinese representatives at any time and in any place. To date, China has refused to open a dialogue.

The travels of the Dalai Lama have also made the Tibetan leader one of the best known and most respected spiritual figures in the modern era. As people all over the world came to know the lama, they realized the richness of his message beyond the appeal for Tibet, such as his teachings concerning peace, compassion, inner peace, and the environment. He was soon an honored guest and lecturer, with often startling insights into global issues and crises, and has been largely responsible for the marked increase in the popularity of Tibetan Buddhism in the

West and the heightened appreciation around the world for Tibetan art, music, and culture. His efforts on behalf of peace and the environment have earned him many awards, including the 1989 Prix de Memoire, the Palketta Award, the Albert Schweitzer Humanitarian Award, the Peace Medal, and the Raoul Wallenberg Congressional Human Rights Award. In presenting the Raoul Wallenberg Award in 1989, United States congressman Tom Lantos observed: "His Holiness the Dalai Lama's courageous struggle has distinguished him as a leading proponent of human rights and world peace."

Today, the Dalai Lama continues to travel to any country where he finds welcome and where his teachings about Buddhism, human rights, and the paths to inner peace will be heard. A prolific author, he has written extensively on Tibetan Buddhism but is perhaps best known for his two autobiographies, *My Land and My People* (1964) and *Freedom in Exile* (1990). Though he is a Nobel laureate, a beloved and influential religious leader, and, for Tibetans, the living incarnation of the Buddha of Compassion, he remains in all essentials exactly what he describes himself to be: "a simple Buddhist monk, no more, no less," living in his residence, a small cottage, in Dharamsala.

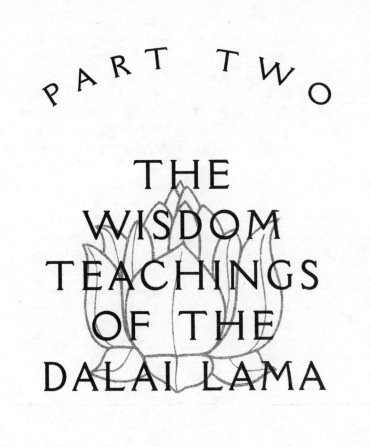

PART TWO

THE WISDOM TEACHINGS OF THE DALAI LAMA

Section One

DHARMA
AND
RELIGION

Words of Truth

O Buddhas, Bodhisattvas, and disciples
Of the past, the present, and the future
Who possess remarkable qualities
As immeasurably vast as the ocean
Who hold all helpless and sentient beings
As though they were your only child
I pray that you might consider the justice of this
    anguished cry.

All of the Buddha's teachings eradicate the pain
Of a cyclic existence and selfish peace.
May the teachings flourish, bringing prosperity and
    happiness
Throughout this wide world.
O Keepers of the Dharma: scholars and realized
    practitioners
May your ten practices of virtue triumph.

Humble sentient beings are tormented
By sufferings without end
Dominated utterly
By negative actions seemingly intense and eternal.
May all their fears of intolerable war
Of famine and disease be quieted
That they might breathe with freedom in an ocean
Of happiness and well-being.
And especially pious beings

From the Land of Snows who, by various means,
Are slain without mercy by hordes of barbarians
Who belong to the cause of darkness,
Permit the strength of your compassion,
For the sake of goodness
To ease the flow of blood and tears.

Those objects of compassion, relentlessly cruel,
Who are deluded by demons of emotion
And who without remorse destroy others and
     themselves,
May they find the eye of wisdom
Knowing what ought to be done and what ought to be
     forsaken
And dwell in the glory of friendship and love.

May this wish from the heart for the total freedom
For all Tibet
Which has been awaited for so long
Come to pass spontaneously.
Grant, I pray, the chance to relish
The joyous celebration of spiritual and temporal rule
     united.

O protector Chenrezig, take care with compassion
Those who have endured trials innumerable.
Sacrificing utterly their lives,
Their bodies and their riches
For the sake of the teachings, the believers,
The people, and the nation.

Thus, the Protector Chenrezig made boundless prayers
Before the Buddhas and the Bodhisattvas
To give embrace in fullness to the Land of Snows.
May the fortunate results of these prayers come soon to
     pass
Through the profound interdependence of emptiness
And relative forms.

Combined with the strength of the great compassion
Of the Three Jewels and their Words of Truth
And so through the power
Of the infallible law of cause and effect
May this truthful prayer be fulfilled
And swiftly come to pass.

—Prayer composed by
His Holiness the
XIV Dalai Lama in 1960

Buddhism

Buddhism, with its emphasis on universal love and compassion, impregnated with ideas that are wholly nonviolent and peaceful, offers a means, at once unique and
eternal, for the successful attainment of that state of security and happiness wherefrom man and beast can derive common benefaction. It can rightly be asserted that
loving-kindness and compassion are the two corner-
stones on which the whole edifice of Buddhism stands.
Destruction or injury to life is strictly forbidden. Harming

or destroying any being from the highest to the lowest, from a human to the tiniest insect, must at all costs be avoided. The Blessed One said: "Do not harm others. Just as you feel affection on seeing a dearly beloved person, so should you extend loving-kindness to all creatures."

—*Love and Compassion*

The dividing line between a Buddhist and a non-Buddhist is that the former is someone who takes refuge in the Three Jewels: the Buddha, who is the teacher and the goal to be attained; the Dharma, or the teachings and the path to be realized; and the Sangha, or the holders of the robes and the advanced practitioners of the Dharma. Again, it is very important that this refuge is taken on the basis of a deep understanding of what these Three Jewels signify. Merely to call oneself a Buddhist is of little value; one must have the inner experience of dissatisfaction with mundane existence and the recognition that refuge in the Three Jewels, together with the spiritual practice that this refuge implies, will help transcend this mundane state of being. Then one should gain a firm understanding of the karmic law of cause and effect, and exert oneself at developing harmony with them.

—**Address, 1963**

I go for refuge to the Buddhas, the fully Enlightened Ones, who guide beings by expounding to them the pure, true teachings of the Dharma, which is the fruit of the supreme wisdom derived from their direct experience.

I go for refuge to the Dharma, which affords full transcendence of all suffering and leads to true happiness; for the Dharma connotes the elimination of all negativity and fulfillment of all creative qualities as a result of Wholesome thought and action, functioning through body, speech, and mind.

I go for refuge to the Sangha, the supreme community, whose feet are firmly set on the path to enlightenment. Upon them I place my unswerving reliance for that spiritual assistance of which I stand in need.

—Tantric Meditation

The Buddha's advice simply stated was to avoid harming others and if possible to help them. All other beings are just like us in that they want happiness and dislike suffering. By developing a sense of respect for others and a concern for their welfare, we reduce our own selfishness, which is the source of all problems, and enhance our sense of kindness, which is a natural source of goodness.

—February 1, 1996,
message to Vietnam

The Buddha himself taught different things according to the place, the occasion, and the situation of those who were listening to him. What distinguishes the contemporary situation is that almost the entire array of Buddhist traditions that evolved in different lands are now accessible to anyone who is interested. Especially heartening is that Buddhist women are casting off traditional and outmoded restraints and dedicating themselves to implementing and promoting Buddhist practice.

—"**Greetings to Buddhist Women**"

The essence of Buddhism is kindness, compassion. This is the essence of every religion, but particularly Mahayana Buddhism. I think this is very important and everybody can practice it without deeper faith. Simply, you are a human being; everybody appreciates kindness. In fact, when we grow up, we grow up in the kindness of our parents, and without that sort of kindness we cannot exist. This is very clear because today you find that children who are not brought up within the love of their parents, or where there is a disruption in the family, are later psychologically affected.

—**Address, 1993**

By living in a society we should share the sufferings of our fellow beings and practice compassion and tolerance, not only toward our loved ones but also toward our enemies. This is the test of our strength and practice, and is what Mahayana stresses. Unless we can set an example by our own practice we cannot hope to convince others of the value of Dharma by mere words. We should engage in the same high standards of integrity and sacrifice that we ask of others. . . . Buddhism is always employed to realize the happiness and peace of man and not to convert others or to derive benefit from them.

—*Buddha Dharma and Society*

Our artistic traditions have been a creative force in Asia and at various times have served as an influence, standard, and model for the art of many other countries. Through the exchange and appreciation of Tibet's religious art, we developed common understandings and grew closer to other cultures, and important ideas embodied in our religion spread and took root across Central Asia and beyond. For example, it is impossible to discuss fully Buddhist traditions in India, along the Central Asian Silk Route, or in China, Japan, Korea, and areas of Southeast Asia without reference to rituals, ideas, and artistic forms that evolved in Tibet.

—Address, 1995

Buddhism is atheistic in the sense that a creator God is not accepted; rather, Buddhism presents a view of self-creation, that one's own actions create one's life situations. In this light, it has been said that Buddhism is not a religion, but a science of the mind.

—*Spiritual Contributions to Social Progress*

Whether it be the environment that is inhabited, or the inhabitants, both of them are composed of five or four basic elements. These elements are earth, wind, fire, water, and vacuum, that is, space. About space, in Kalachakra Tantra there is a mention of what is known as the atom of space, particles of space. So that forms the central force of the entire phenomenon. When the entire system of the universe first evolved, it evolved from this central force which is the particle of space, and also a system of universe would dissolve eventually into this particle of the space. So it is on the basis of these five basic elements that there is a very close interrelatedness or interrelation between the habitat that is the natural environment and the inhabitants, the sentient beings living within it. Also, when we talk of the elements there are internal elements which are existent inherently within sentient beings; they are also of different levels—some are subtle and some are gross. So ultimately, according to Buddhist teaching, the innermost subtle consciousness is the sole sort of creator, itself consisting of five elements, very subtle forms of elements. These subtle elements serve as conditions for producing the internal elements which form sentient beings, and that in turn causes the existence or evolution of the external elements. So there is a very close interdependence or interrelationship between the environment and the inhabitants.

—Address, 1996

If you have adopted Buddhism you should not consider yourself a "great Buddhist" and immediately start to do everything differently. A Tibetan proverb states, "Change your mind but leave your appearance as usual."

—Address, 1984

In Buddhism we have relative truth and absolute truth. From the viewpoint of absolute truth, what we feel and experience in our ordinary daily life is all delusion. Of all the various delusions, the sense of discrimination between oneself and others is the worst form, as it creates nothing but unpleasantness for both sides. If we can realize and meditate on ultimate truth, it will cleanse our impurities of mind and thus eradicate the sense of discrimination. This will help to create true love for one another. The search for ultimate truth is, therefore, vitally important.

—*The Two Truths*

The incarnation of a Buddha or Bodhisattva always continues to manifest, not only in human form but sometimes as an insect, as an animal, and so forth. Whether or not a particular being is given the title of "Dalai Lama" depends on whether or not such a process is beneficial. For example, long before the First Dalai Lama there were many other incarnations of the Bodhisattva Avalokiteshvara . . . but these were not given the title of "Dalai Lama." The title "Dalai Lama" was actually first given to the Third Lama, Sönam Gyatso. They then traced back through two previous incarnations and called him and

his two successive incarnations the First and Second Dalai
Lamas.

—Address, 1984

In Tibet, due to differences in the time of translation of
texts from India and the development of lineage formed
by particular teachers, eight distinct schools of Buddhism
arose. Nowadays, four are widely known, Nyingma,
Sakya, Kagyu, and Gelukpa. From the point of view of
their tenets, they are all Madhyamika. From the point of
view of their vehicle, they are all of the Bodhisa Hvayana.
In addition, these four orders are all complete systems of
unified Sutra and Tantra practice, each having the techniques and quintessential instructions necessary for a
person to achieve Buddhahood within one lifetime.

—Lecture of the Nyingma Institute, 1980

The fundamental view or philosophy of Buddhism is that
of "dependent arising." When one talks about the view
of dependent arising, one means that things exist in dependence or that they are imputed depending on something or other. In the case of a physical phenomenon, one
would specify that it exists in dependence on its parts,
whereas nonphysical composite phenomenon would be
described as existing in dependence either on their continuity or an aspect of their continuity.

—*Meeting Points in Science and Spirituality*

ৡ᳅

The Tibetan people are moving to many countries in Asia as well as Europe and North America. And with interest in Tibetan Buddhism growing throughout the world, it must be recognized now more than ever that Tibetan Buddhism and the Tibetan people can play a truly international role in world cultures. I have always felt that the Buddhist culture can make positive contribution to the rest of the world, because of its principal stress on compassion and, especially in the Mahayana tradition, by its profession of nonviolence in various human activities.

—Address, 1995

ৡ᳅

In past centuries, there have been many learned teachers who have laid down various paths to the realization of Truth. Among them, Lord Buddha is one, and my study of Buddhism has led me to form the opinion that, despite the differences in the names and forms used by the various religions, the ultimate truth to which they point is the same.

—*The Two Truths*

ৡ᳅

Tibetan culture is rich mainly due to Buddha's teaching, I think. Central to Buddha's teaching is seeing the equality among humanity and the importance of equality of all sentient beings. Whether you are a Buddhist or not, this is something important to know and to understand.

—Address, 1984

🦎

Whether one practices Mahayana or Hinayana, the "Cause Vehicle," or the "Effect Vehicle of Mahayana," each of these is a valid form of the glorious Teaching of the Lord Buddha. Sometimes it may happen that a person who has not made a proper study of, or not yet fully realized, all these doctrines of the Blessed One will find himself puzzled by what appear to be some elementary contradictions between the concepts of Mahayana and Hinayana, or of Sutra and Tantra. For indeed the Buddha Dharma does have different and contradictory aspects, namely permissive and prohibitive precepts, within the vast concourse of its philosophical system. This gives rise to different and varying forms of practice and conduct. Only by delving deeply into these seeming contradictions, after equipping oneself by a deep study and by clearly comprehending the body of Lord Buddha's teaching in all its aspects, will one acquire a comprehensive knowledge of the methods and systems of its procedure and practice.

—Combining the Three Vehicles

🦎

Our compassionate and nonviolent Buddhist culture has much to offer to the rest of the world, and especially to China and the Chinese people, to whom Buddhism is not an alien religion.

—Address, 1995

🦎

Buddhism is one of the many religions which teaches us to be less selfish and more compassionate. It teaches us to be humane, altruistic, and to think of others in the way we think of ourselves. Our daily thoughts and actions should be directed toward the benefit of others. Mahayana emphasizes self-sacrifice and the development of altruism while Hinayana teaches us the importance of not harming others. The practice of Buddhism in essence is, therefore, not to harm others under any circumstances, and help others as much as possible.

—*Buddha Dharma and Society*

I try to make a distinction between the essence of Buddhism and the cultural part of Tibetan Buddhism. The essential part is more or less the same everywhere, while the cultural part may change from country to country. So I think it may not succeed if a Westerner adopts Tibetan Buddhism in its complete form, as practiced by Tibetans, in a Western society. It will help if we take the essence and adopt it to the existing conditions.

—Address, 1986

It is vitally important to eliminate the cause of suffering and to acquire the cause of happiness. However, to attain any kind of lasting happiness, we must diligently accumulate its causes, and to eliminate suffering, we must use appropriate means to prevent the arising of causes. These two purposes can be accomplished only by full recognition of the true causes of joy and sorrow. To accomplish these two purposes, it is useful to rely upon and show the utmost confidence in the Buddhadharma, a confidence that gains strength from the most probing analysis undertaken in the light of inquiry and reason.

—*Tantric Meditation*

🎋

In all of Buddhism and especially in Mahayana, the benefiting of others is heavily stressed. In this context Shantideva [an eighth-century Buddhist saint] says in *Venturing into the Deeds of a Bodhisattva*, "First investigate what is acceptable and what is unacceptable to the people (of the society in which you live); then avoid what is unacceptable." Of course, you must first consider whether or not what is acceptable and unacceptable is in contradiction with the Dharma. If the social norm does not contradict Dharma you should try to live in accordance with it.

—**Address, 1984**

🎋

Converting other people to Buddhism is not my concern. I am interested in how we Buddhists can contribute to human society. The Buddha gave us an example of contentment and tolerance, through serving others unselfishly. I believe that his teaching and example can still contribute to global peace and individual happiness.

—**"Greetings to Buddhist Women"**

🎋

The Dalai Lama, from the field of Buddhism, at least in Mahayana Buddhism, not only belongs to Tibet but also to wherever Mahayana teaching is practiced. Like the head of the Catholics, the Dalai Lama's personal nationality is not of much importance. The institution somehow belongs everywhere. In ancient times also, Mongolians and a large number of Chinese took the Dalai Lama as their own head. There is no feeling at all that the Dalai Lama is not Chinese or Mongolian but Tibetan.

—*Address, 1984*

One is called a Bodhisattva when one's mind is filled with the pure compassion and equanimity which proceed from Bodhimind. As whatever we do in our everyday life results from the functioning of our minds, ultimate peace and Buddhahood are the result of Bodhimind and compassion. The Lord Buddha has said: ''Bodhimind is the seed of Dharma [Teaching].''

—*Love and Compassion*

In Buddhism, there are three categories: the so-called Hinayana or lesser vehicle, Mahayana or greater vehicle, and Tantrayana. The followers of Hinayana aim for the salvation of oneself while those of Mahayana aim for the liberation or salvation for entire sentient beings. In these two the difference is only in the motivation. Naturally, as soon as one thinks about others, then the most important thing is compassion.

—*Address, 1986*

Reflect upon the causes of our sufferings, which is negative karma and delusion. Of these, delusion is the greater foe, for it is delusions that activate our negative karma. Thus, they bring misery to every living being. These delusions, the mental defilements that wreak the most fearful harm, are the true enemy of all living beings.

—*Tantric Meditation*

A Christian could learn certain methods from Buddhism. There are already some Westerners who adopt certain Buddhist methods for their own practices, certain techniques to improve their mental alertness. Then there are Westerners who remain in Western society but at the same time practice Buddhism, especially Tibetan Buddhism. I think we will eventually know from their experiences the contribution of Tibetan Buddhism to Western society.

—**Address, 1986**

In Christian teaching, suffering has some powerful meaning, doesn't it? For example, Jesus took the suffering himself. Now that, you see, was not in the ordinary sense, but something very meaningful. Now in Buddhist tradition, we have every right to avoid, to overcome suffering, but when the suffering actually happens, then instead of being discouraged or mentally distressed, you simply utilize that occasion in such a way that it will minimize your mental disturbance, and for a long run you develop a certain kind of motivation that will help you to gain more virtue.

—*Address, 1985*

In that supreme mind which shines on all beings,
　　Bringing aid and benefit to every sentient being,
　　I profoundly rejoice with the utmost veneration.
　　I rejoice in the thought of enlightenment and in the Dharma,
　　That ocean of happiness for every sentient being
　　Wherein abides the welfare of all that lives.

—*Tantric Meditation*

Buddhism is very sophisticated philosophically and strongly stresses rationality. In this sense it is very modern in its sensitivity and outlook. There is a basis here for cooperation and dialogue with Western sciences. Every religion has its own character and atmosphere. I truly respect Christianity and the contribution it has made and continues to make to world civilization. But no one religion is appropriate for all types of people. Just as Buddhism is not best for everyone, Christianity is not appropriate to all types of dispositions.

—*Address, 1986*

Meditation and Inner Peace

Everybody loves to talk about calm and peace whether in a family, national, or international context, but without *inner* peace how can we make real peace? World peace through hatred and force is impossible. Even in the case of individuals, there is no possibility to feel happiness through anger. If in a difficult situation one becomes disturbed internally, overwhelmed by mental discomfort, then external things will not help at all. However, if despite external difficulties or problems, internally one's attitude is of love, warmth and kindheartedness, then problems can be faced and accepted easily.

—*Compassion in Global Politics*

Material progress alone is not sufficient to achieve an ideal society. Even in countries where great external progress has been made, mental problems have increased, causing additional hardships. No amount of legislation or coercion can accomplish the well-being of society, for this depends upon the internal attitude of the people who compose it.

—Address, 1981

Basically, we all cherish tranquillity. For example, when spring comes, the days grow longer, there is more sunshine, the grass and trees come alive and everything is fresh. People feel happy. In autumn, one leaf falls, then another, then all the beautiful flowers die until we are surrounded by bare, naked plants. We do not feel so joyful. Why is this? Because deep down, we desire constructive, fruitful growth and dislike things collapsing, dying, or being destroyed. Every destructive action goes against our basic nature: building, being constructive, is the human way.

—"Universal Responsibility and
Our Global Environment"

Unless our minds are stable and calm, no matter how comfortable our physical condition may be, they will give us no pleasure. Therefore, the key to a happy life, now and in the future, is to develop a happy mind.

—"The True Expression of
Nonviolence Is Compassion"

If striving thus were really productive of permanent happiness, then among the many people in this world endowed with power, wealth, and friendship, there would surely be some blessed with a large measure of real and lasting happiness. But in truth, though there are indeed relative differences in the amount and intensity of happiness enjoyed, every single one of us—be he a ruler or warrior, be he rich, middle-class, or poor—is subject to all sorts of physical and mental suffering, especially torments of the mind.

—Tantric Meditation

And, you know in our day-to-day life if, inside, you possess good qualities such as compassion or spiritual forgiveness or wider perspective—these things are there—then, no matter what the circumstances, even if you are surrounded by hostile attitudes, the external factor will not affect the internal peace of the mind. So therefore, the compassion is a source of happiness. On the other hand, in one day if you have some ill-feeling or hatred there, then the whole day, no matter what good facility is there or no matter what good friends are with you, that day you will not be happy. So therefore, the inner, mental attitude is, I think, the major factor for happiness and unhappiness.

—Address, 1995

For any change, any movement in the human community—the initiative must come from individuals. So if an individual human being eventually becomes a nice, calm, peaceful person, then it automatically brings some kind of positive atmosphere, and you have a happy family. Once two parents are warmhearted and peaceful and calm persons, then their children eventually develop that kind of behavior. So, therefore I think the individual, the happy individual human being, is very important.

—"Compassion, the Basis for
Human Happiness"

To make the mind docile, it is essential for us to discipline and control it well. Speech and bodily activities which accompany mental processes must not be allowed to run on in an indiscreet, unbridled, random way. Just as a trainer disciplines and calms a wild and willful steed by subjecting it to skillful and prolonged training, so must the wild, wandering, random activities of body and speech be tamed to make them docile, righteous, and skillful. Therefore the Teachings of the Lord Buddha comprise three graded categories, that is . . . Shila (Training in Higher Conduct), Samadhi (Training in Higher Meditation), and Prajna (Training in Higher Wisdom), all of them for disciplining the mind.

—*Happiness, Karma, and the Mind*

If we live our lives continually motivated by anger and hatred, even our physical health deteriorates.

—"The True Expression of
Nonviolence Is Compassion"

We human beings have a developed brain and limitless potential. Since even wild animals can gradually be trained with patience, the human mind also can gradually be trained, step by step. If you test these practices with patience, you can come to know this through your own experience. If someone who easily gets angry tries to control his or her anger, in time it can be controlled. The same is true for a very selfish person; first that person must realize the faults of a selfish motivation and the benefit in being less selfish. Having realized this, one trains in it, trying to control the bad side and develop the good.

—**Address, 1980**

I believe that the very purpose of life is to be happy. From the moment of birth, every human being wants happiness and does not want suffering. Neither social conditioning nor education nor ideology affect this. From the very core of our being, we simply desire contentment. Therefore, it is important to discover what will bring about the greatest degree of happiness. Hence we should devote our most serious efforts to bring about mental peace.

—*Disarmament, Peace, and Compassion*

We are trying to get peace or happiness from outside, from money or power. But real peace, tranquillity, should come from within.

—**Address, 1984**

In the case of such global issues as the conservation of the earth, and indeed in taking all problems, the human mind is the key factor. Whether they are problems of economics, international relations, science, technology, medicine, or ecology, though these issues seem to be beyond any one individual's capacity, where the problem begins and where the answer must first be sought is within. In order to change the external situation we must first change within ourselves. If we want a beautiful garden, we must first have a blueprint in the imagination, a vision. Then that idea can be implemented and the external garden can be materialized.

—*Caring for the Earth*

Our day-to-day life, especially in the future, the very long future, very much depends on hope. There is no guarantee about the future, but one based on hope. Hope means something good. Nobody hopes for something bad. Therefore, the very purpose of our life is happiness: in order to achieve happier days, happier weeks, happier years, happier family, happier human community. Since the mental attitude is a major factor, I think we should pay more attention to inner development.

—*Address, 1995*

Those points which I mentioned here, I hope you think over them. And if you feel there is something beneficial, then please experiment in your daily life. Through experiment if you find no result, then forget it. No problem. And also those people who feel these points are nonsense, have no meaning, then just forget, no problem. But if you feel something is there, then please implement. Try to experiment. That's very important. You see, positive things do not come by nature. For positive things we have to make an effort. We must make the effort. Nobody, no one else, can do that. So everyone, hope for a better future, a happier future, if that is our wish. The present generation must make every effort. It is our responsibility.

—Address, 1995

Now here is part of my own little experience: The most important factor for mental peace is, I believe—of course there are some other factors, some other qualities—but I think one of the very important factors is human compassion, affection, sense of caring. Let me explain what is the meaning of compassion. Usually, the concept of compassion or love is something like closeness or a feeling toward your friend. And also, sometimes, compassion means a feeling of pity—that is wrong. Compassion, or love in which someone looks down on another—that's not genuine compassion. Genuine compassion must be acting on the basis of respect, and the realization or recognition that others also, just like myself, have the right to be happy or work on suffering. And yet suffering is there. We should therefore develop some kind of genuine concern, a real sense of concern.

—"Compassion, the Basis
for Human Happiness"

🌿

Inner tranquillity comes from the development of love and compassion. The more we care for the happiness of others, the greater is our own sense of well-being. Cultivating a close, warmhearted feeling for others automatically puts the mind at ease and opens our inner door. It helps remove whatever fears or insecurities we may have and gives us the strength to cope with any obstacles we encounter. It is the principal source of success in life. Since we are not solely material creatures, it is a mistake to place all our hopes for happiness on external development alone. Instead, we should consider our origins and nature to discover what we require.

—*Disarmament, Peace, and Compassion*

🌿

One question is whether we can really change our minds. Or whether we can develop this positive mind, and whether we can reduce a negative mind. The answer is definitely yes, and the reason is quite simple. The mind has no form, no shape. Even the physical thing is like rubber, and very difficult to control, isn't it? It is flexible, even too flexible. So the mind also seems anyway very difficult to control. But at the same time if you make constant effort, as time goes by, you can see a change.

—*Address, 1995*

🌿

There are two kinds of satisfaction or happiness: one mainly through mental peace; another physical comfort.

So obviously material development provides us physical comfort, and through that you may also, you see, get some kind of mental satisfaction. . . . Mental satisfaction comes mainly through mental attitude. So now, between these two the mental satisfaction, which comes through mental attitude, purely mental attitude, is stronger; it is superior. So therefore, you see, there is no point to neglect that part of our experience.

—"The Need to Balance Spiritual and Material Values"

When we talk about the inner world, there are a lot of different thoughts, or different minds. Among these hundreds of thoughts, some are very useful to us, very positive. Some are negative. Now, here you see the definition or demarcation of positive and negative means those thoughts and actions which ultimately bring happiness; that is positive. Those thoughts and actions which ultimately bring suffering, that is negative. Nothing else. Therefore, the different thoughts or minds are positive and negative. It is thus very, very useful to analyze these different minds or different thoughts. Then, through effort, or on the basis of clear events, we see something useful or something harmful. Then, through mental training you can increase these positive thoughts and can reduce negative thoughts. I can tell you with full conviction, through effort we can change our mental attitude.

—Address, 1995

୬༵

Mental peace cannot be injected by any doctor; no market can sell mental peace or happiness. With millions and millions of rupees you can buy anything, but if you go to a supermarket and say I want peace of mind, then people will laugh. And if you ask a doctor, I want genuine peace of mind, not a dull one, you might get a sleeping pill, or some injection. Although you may get some rest, the rest is not in the right sense, is it? So if you want genuine mental peace or mental tranquillity, the doctor cannot provide it. A machine like the computer, however sophisticated it may be, cannot provide you mental peace.

—**Address, 1996**

୬༵

At a time when people are so conscious of maintaining their physical health by controlling their diets, exercising, and so forth, it makes sense to try to cultivate the corresponding positive mental attitudes too.

—**"The True Expression of Nonviolence Is Compassion"**

୬༵

Our goal is happiness. And I believe the very purpose of our life is happiness. Whether we believe in a previous life or not, whether we believe in a next life or not, the very existence of this life I feel is meant for happiness.

—**Address, 1995**

It is easier to meditate than to actually do something for others. Sometimes I feel that to merely meditate on compassion is to take the passive option. Our meditation should form the basis for action, for seizing the opportunity to do something. The meditator's motivation, his sense of universal responsibility, should be expressed in deeds.

—"The True Expression of
Nonviolence Is Compassion"

Mental peace must come from the mind. So everyone wants happiness, pleasure. Now, compare physical pleasure and physical pain with mental pain or mental pleasure, and you will find that the mind is superior, more effective, and more dominant. Therefore it is worthwhile to increase mental peace through certain methods. In order to do that it is important to know more about the mind. That also, I always feel, is very important. I think that is all.

—Address, 1996

Good Heart

We need human qualities such as moral scruples, compassion, and humility. In recognition of human frailty and weakness, these qualities are accessible only through forceful individual development in a conducive social milieu so that a more humane world will come into being as an ultimate goal. Self-realization that materialism does not foster the growth of morals, compassion, and humility should be innately created. The functional importance of religious and social institutions toward promoting these qualities thus assumes a serious responsibility, and all efforts should be concentrated sincerely in fulfilling these needs.

—*Dharma and Politics*

The development of a kind heart, or feeling of closeness for all human beings, does not involve any kind of the religiosity we normally associate with it. It is not just for people who believe in religion; it is for everyone, irrespective of race, religion, or of any political affiliation. It is for anybody who considers himself first and foremost a member of the human family and who sees things in larger terms.

—Address, 1973

I am a religious person, and from my viewpoint all things first originate in the mind. Things and events depend heavily on motivation. A real sense of appreciation of humanity, compassion, and love are the key points. If we develop a good heart, then whether the field is science, agriculture, or politics, since motivation is so very important, these will all improve. A good heart is both important and effective in daily life. If in a small family, even without children, the members have a warm heart to each other, a peaceful atmosphere will be created. However, if one of the persons feels angry, immediately the atmosphere in the house becomes tense. Despite good food or a nice television set, you will lose peace and calm.

—*Compassion in Global Politics*

In the correlation between ethics and politics, should deep moral convictions form the guideline for the political practitioner, man and his society will reap far-reaching benefits. It is an absurd assumption that religion and morality have no place in politics and that a man of religion and a believer in morality should seclude himself as a hermit. These ideas lack proper perspective vis-à-vis man's relation to his society and the role of politics in our lives.

—*Dharma and Politics*

Once you have pure and sincere motivation, all the rest follows. You can develop this right attitude toward others on the basis of kindness, love, and respect, and on the clear realization of the oneness of all human beings. This is important because others benefit by this motivation as much as anything we do. Then, with a pure heart, you can carry on any work . . . and your profession becomes a real instrument to help the human community.

—*Address, 1984*

To pursue growth properly, we need to renew our commitment to human values in many fields. Political life, of course, requires an ethical foundation, but science and religion as well should be pursued from a moral basis. Without it, scientists cannot distinguish between beneficial technologies and those which are merely expedient.

—**"Universal Responsibility and Our Global Environment"**

I believe happiness comes from kindness. Happiness cannot come from hatred or anger. Nobody can say, "Today I am happy because this morning I was very angry." On the contrary, people feel uneasy and sad and say, "Today I am not very happy because I lost my temper this morning." So you see this fact is something natural. Through kindness, whether at our own level or at the national and international level, through mutual understanding and through mutual respect we will get peace, we will get happiness, and we will get genuine satisfaction. It is very difficult to achieve peace and harmony through competition and hatred, so the practice of kindness is very, very important and very, very valuable in human society.

—**Address, 1963**

In order to increase the sense of cherishing others, it is first important to think about the faults of cherishing ourselves and the good qualities of cherishing others. If we cherish others, then both others and ourselves, both deeply and superficially, will be happy. Whether in terms of the family or of the family of nations as a whole world, if we take the cherishing of others as the very basis of policy for our format, then we will be able to succeed in our common effort.

—**Address, 1982**

A good mind, a good heart, warm feelings—these are the most important things. If you don't have such a good mind, you yourself cannot function. You cannot be happy, and so also your own kin, your own mate or children, or neighbors and so forth won't be happy either.

—**Address, 1981**

Strong moral ethics are as concomitantly crucial to a man of politics as they are to a man of religion, for dangerous consequences are foreseen when our politicians and those who rule forget their moral principles and convictions. Irrespective of whether we are a believer or an agnostic, whether we believe in God or karma, moral ethics is a code which everyone is able to pursue.

—*Dharma and Politics*

And thus from nation to nation and continent to continent, everyone's mind becomes disturbed, people lose happiness. But then, on the other hand, if you have a good attitude, a good, good heart, then the opposite is true.

—Address, 1981

The prime mover of every human action is the motivation or the determination. First, our motivation should be simple and sincere. Whether we achieve the goal or not does not matter so long as our motivation is very sincere and we make an attempt. Finally, even if we fail to achieve our goal, we won't regret making the effort. If our motivation is not sincere, even if the objective is achieved the person will not be so happy or satisfied deep down. So motivation is very important.

—"Universal Responsibility and the Inner Environment"

Most of the good or beneficial effects that come about in the world are based on an attitude of cherishing others. The opposite is also true. When we cherish ourselves more than others, both superficially and deeply, we produce various types of suffering, both for ourselves and for those around us. Therefore, we need to make an effort at the root of this goodness, that is to say, this good heart, warm heart.

—Address, 1982

By showing concern for other people's welfare, sharing other people's suffering, and by helping other people, ultimately one will benefit. If one thinks only of oneself and forgets about others, ultimately one will lose. This also is something like nature's law. I think it is quite simple. If you do not show a smile to other people, and show some kind of bad look or like that, the other side will also give a similar response. Isn't that right? If you show other people a very sincere and open attitude, there will also be a similar response. So it is quite simple logic. Everybody wants friends and does not want enemies. The proper way to create friends is through a warm heart and not simply money or power. Friends of power and friends of money are something different. These are not friends. A true friend should be a real friend of the heart, isn't it so? I am telling people that those friends who come to you when you have money and power are not your true friends but friends of money and power. Because as soon as your money and power disappear, those friends are also ready to say good-bye, bye-bye. So you see these friends are not reliable.

—Address, 1996

Usually you allow kindness toward family members. This kindness is inspired by affection, desire. Because of that, when the object of your compassion changes in aspect, becomes a little rough, then your own feeling changes also. That kind of compassion or love is not right. Therefore, it is necessary in the beginning to train these good attitudes.

—**Address, 1981**

So, any human action, whether the result is positive or negative largely depends on motivation. If the motivation is sincere, then every human action can be positive— including political initiatives. If our motivation is not adequate, not pure, even religion becomes smeared. So, therefore, things ultimately depend upon proper motivation. I consider the important thing is unshakable determination based upon a genuine sense of brotherhood and sisterhood or a sense of Universal Responsibility based on human compassion or affection. That is the proper mental approach; our goal may not be achieved so easily this way—it may take more time and may face many obstacles. I think right from the beginning we must adopt that kind of attitude.

—**"Universal Responsibility and the Inner Environment"**

There is no need to mention the great difference between the amount of satisfaction there is in just oneself being happy and the amount of satisfaction there is in an infinite number of people being happy.

Address, 1980

The world, unfortunately, is not pure; there are lots of negative forces. For thirty-three years I have been telling my fellow Tibetans that we should hope for the best but at the same time prepare with optimism for the worst. An optimistic attitude is the key factor for success. Right from the beginning, if you hold a pessimistic attitude, even small things may not be achieved. Therefore, to remain optimistic all the time is very important.

—"**Universal Responsibility and the
Inner Environment**"

When one gives one's kindness for the sake of getting something back in return, for the sake of getting a good name, for the sake of causing other people to like oneself, if the motive is for self, then this would not be really a Bodhisattva deed. Therefore, one-pointedness points to giving only for the sake of helping others.

—**Address, 1983**

Sometimes we humans put too much importance on secondary matters, such as differences of political systems or economic systems or race. There seem to be many discriminations due to these differences. But comparatively basic human well-being is not based on these things. So I always try to understand the real human values. All these different philosophies or religious systems are supposed to serve human happiness. But there is something wrong when there is too much emphasis on these secondary matters, these differences in systems which are supposed to serve human happiness.

—Address, 1981

It is necessary to make a distinction between external enemies and internal ones. External enemies are not permanent; if you respect him, the enemy will become your friend. But there is one enemy who is always an enemy, with whom you should never compromise; that is the enemy inside your heart. You cannot change all these bad thoughts into your friend, but you have to confront and control them.

—Address, 1992

If you want more friends and a friendly atmosphere, you must create the basis for them. Whether the other's response will be positive or not, first you must create some kind of common ground. Then if the other's response is still negative, you act accordingly. So first, you see, we must create the possibility to react in a friendly manner.

—"Compassion, the Basis for Human Happiness"

Above all, we must put others before us and keep others in our mind constantly: the self must be placed last. All our doings and thinkings must be motivated by compassion for others. The way to acquire that kind of outlook is that we must accept the simple fact that whatever we desire is also desired by others.

—Address, 1973

Peaceful living is about trusting those on whom we depend and caring for those who depend on us. Even if only a few individuals try to create mental peace and happiness within themselves and act responsibly and kind-heartedly toward others, they will have a positive influence in their community.

—Address, 1994

Every being wants happiness, no suffering. If we adopt a self-centered approach to life by which we attempt to use others for our own self-interest, we might be able to gain temporary benefit, but in the long run we will not succeed in achieving even our personal happiness, and hope for a next life is out of the question.

—Address, 1992

The reason why we seek to behave in a good manner is that it's from good behavior that good fruits are derived. So, the basic reason is that one wants happiness and doesn't want suffering, and on the basis of that, one enters into good actions and avoids bad actions. Goodness and badness of actions are determined on the basis of the goodness and the badness of their fruits.

—**Address, 1981**

Buddha showed that purifying the mind is not easy. It takes a lot of time and hard work. But this is also true of any human enterprise. You need tremendous willpower and determination right from the start, accepting that there will be many obstacles, and resolving that despite them all you will continue until you have attained your goal.

—**"Greetings to Buddhist Women"**

If one assumes a humble attitude, one's own good qualities will increase. Whereas if one is proud, one will become jealous of others, one will become angry with others, and one will look down on others. Due to that, there will be unhappiness in society.

—**Address, 1981**

As human beings we have good qualities as well as bad ones. Now, anger, attachment, jealousy, hatred, are the bad side; these are the real enemy. From a certain point of view, our real enemy, the true troublemaker, is inside. So these bad thoughts remain active, and as long as you have these, it is difficult to attain mental peace. . . . My suggestion or advice is very simple; that is, to have a sincere heart.

—**Address, 1994**

As a human being, kindness, a warm heart, is very important. . . . If you have this basic quality of kindness or good heart, then all other things, education, ability, will go in the right direction. If you have a bad heart, then knowledge or ability are used in the wrong direction; instead of helping others, it makes trouble.

—**Address, 1993**

Whether we are rich or poor, educated or uneducated, whatever our nationality, color, social status, or ideology may be, the purpose of our lives is to be happy.

—**"The True Expression of
Nonviolence Is Compassion"**

Every man has the basis of good. Not only human beings, you can find it among animals or insects, for instance, when we treat a dog or horse lovingly.

—**Address, 1992**

If even one person cannot stand suffering, what need is there to mention how all people can't stand suffering?

Therefore, it is a mistake if one uses others' welfare. Thus one should use whatever capacities of body, speech, and mind one has for the benefit of others: That is right. Thus it is necessary to generate an altruistic mind and wish that the welfare of others is increased through their achievement of happiness and through their getting rid of suffering.

—Address, 1981

Love

As one brought up in the Mahayana Buddhist tradition, I feel that love and compassion are the moral fabric of world peace. Let me first define what I mean by compassion. When you have pity or compassion for a very poor person, you are showing sympathy because he or she is poor; your compassion is based on altruistic considerations. On the other hand, love toward your wife, your husband, your children, or a close friend is usually based on attachment. When your attachment changes, your kindness also changes; it may disappear. This is not true love. Real love is not based on attachment, but on altruism. In this case your compassion will remain as a human response to suffering as long as beings continue to suffer.

—Compassion in Global Politics

Do we not agree that love plays an important part in human life? It consoles when one is helpless and distressed, and it consoles when one is old and lonely. It is a dynamic force that we should develop and use, but often tend to neglect, particularly in our prime years, when we experience a false sense of security. The rationale for loving others is the recognition of the simple fact that every living being has the same right to and the same desire for happiness and not suffering, and the consideration that you as the one individual are one life unit as compared with the multitude of others in their ceaseless quest for happiness.

—**Address, 1973**

Without love we could not survive. Human beings are social creatures, and a concern for each other is the very basis of our life together.

—**"The True Expression of Nonviolence Is Compassion"**

Love is the center of human life.

—**Address, 1981**

The feeling of a mother for her child is a classic example of love. For the safety, protection, and welfare of her children, a mother is ready to sacrifice her very life. Recognizing this, children should be grateful to their mothers and express their gratitude by performing virtuous deeds. In

the same way, a person motivated by the thought of Bodhimind strives with all his might for the welfare of every
sentient being, whether it be a human or a beast or a fowl
of land or sea. At the same time, he will treat all the beings as he treats his mother. In repayment of her mater-
nal love, it will be his constant endeavor to do only what
is benevolent. In short, the cultivation of compassion and
loving kindness for all sentient beings will bring peace
and happiness to oneself and others. Ill-will, malice, and
malevolent acts will only be a source of suffering to all.

—Love and Compassion

Right from the moment of our birth, we are under the
care and kindness of our parents. And then later on in our
life, when we are oppressed by sickness and become old,
we are again dependent, on the kindness of others. And
since at the beginning and end of our lives we are so dependent on others' kindness, how can it be in the middle
that we neglect kindness toward others?

—Address, 1981

Christians say love for God, love for neighbor, love for
fellow being. This is my personal interpretation of Christianity. And just as you have love for God, love for your
neighbor, so the purpose of having love for God is to be
able to make yourself close to God. If you are close to
God, you have a motive to listen to His voice, and His
voice or teaching is that we should love one another. Basi-

cally the most important thing is this love for others. In Buddhism also every emphasis is on love for others.

—Address, 1973

At the time of our birth, we have neither religion nor ideology nor culture. We acquire or learn about these later in our lives. But I believe that no one is born free from the need for love. No material object, however beautiful or valuable, can make us feel loved, because our deeper identity and true character lie in the subjective nature of the mind.

—*Disarmament, Peace, and Compassion*

Love is a simple practice yet it is very beneficial for the individual who practices it as well as for the community in which he lives, for the nation, and for the whole world.

—Address, 1980

The key to creating a better and more peaceful world is the development of love and compassion for others.

—"Human Rights and Universal Responsibility"

Love and kindness are always appropriate. Whether or not you believe in rebirth, you will need love in this life.

If we have love, there is hope to have real families, real brotherhood, real equanimity, real peace. If the mind of love is lost, if you continue to see other beings as enemies, then no matter how much knowledge or education you have, no matter how much material progress is made, only suffering and confusion will ensue. Beings will continue to deceive and overpower one another. Basically, everyone exists in the very nature of suffering, so to abuse or mistrust each other is futile. The foundation of all spiritual practice is love. That you practice this well is my only request. Of course, to be able to do so in all situations will take time, but you should not lose courage. If we wish happiness for mankind, love is the only way.

—Address, 1980

If you have love and compassion toward all sentient beings, particularly toward your enemy, that is true love and compassion. Now, the kind of love or compassion that you have toward your friends, your wife, and your children is essentially not true kindness. That is attachment. That kind of love cannot be infinite.

—Address, 1980

This need for cooperation can only strengthen humankind, because it helps us to recognize that the most secure foundation for a new world order is not simply broader political and economic alliances, but each individual's genuine practice of love and compassion. These qualities are the ultimate source of human happiness, and our need for them lies at the very core of our being.

—"**Human Rights and Universal Responsibility**"

I always remember, when I visit a church, Mary carrying Jesus Christ as a small baby. That to me is a symbol of affection. So, you see, then obviously those children whose homes have love and affection are better, healthier, normal, and sturdy. Where children lack human affection and love, physical development is sometimes difficult as is study. So then I think the most important thing is that those children who had difficulties at an early age growing under the lack of human love and affection will find it difficult to show other humans love and compassion. And that's a great tragedy, a great tragedy.

—"**Compassion, the Basis for
Human Happiness**"

We can extend . . . love by regarding ourselves as a member of the human family in an interdependent world, relying on others for our welfare and comfort. Also, if we have a kind and loving heart we will win more friends. We will feel better. Such a motivation may be selfish. But if we are selfish with wisdom, then we will realize the need to love others, near and far, even our enemies.

—**Address, 1982**

If we stop to think, compared to the numerous acts of kindness on which we depend and which we take so much for granted, acts of hostility are relatively few. To see the truth of this we only need to observe the love and affection parents shower on their children and the many other acts of loving and caring that we take for granted.

—"**The True Expression of Nonviolence Is Compassion**"

One of the basic points is kindness. With kindness, with love and compassion, with this feeling that is the essence of brotherhood, sisterhood, one will have inner peace.

—**Address, 1981**

If we cherish others, then both others and ourselves, both deeply and superficially, will be happy. Whether in terms of the family or of the family of nations as a whole world, if we take the cherishing of others as the very basis of policy for our format, then we will be able to succeed in our common effort. Most of the good or beneficial effects that come about in the world are based on an attitude of cherishing others. The opposite is also true. When we cherish ourselves more than others, both superficially and deeply, we produce various types of suffering, both for ourselves and for those around us.

—**Address, 1983**

Compassion

Genuine compassion is unbiased, should be unbiased.

—"Compassion, the Basis for
Human Happiness"

The essence of the Mahayana School, which we try to practice, is compassion. In Mahayana Buddhism you sacrifice yourself in order to attain salvation for the sake of other beings.

—Address, 1963

Faced with the challenge of establishing genuine world peace and preserving the bountiful earth, what can we do? Beautiful words are no longer enough. We should instead embark on the difficult task of building an attitude of love and compassion within ourselves. Compassion is, by nature, peaceful and gentle, but it is also very powerful. Some may dismiss it as impractical and unrealistic, but I believe its practice is the true source of success. It is a sign of true inner strength. To achieve it we do not need to become religious, nor do we need any ideology. All that is necessary is for us to develop our basic human qualities.

—*Disarmament, Peace, and Compassion*

Compassion for others (as opposed to self) is one of the central teachings of Mahayana Buddhism. In this connection I would like to quote a verse which conveys the message:

> If you are unable to exchange your happiness
> For the suffering of other beings,
> You have no hope of attaining Buddhahood,
> Or even of happiness in this present life.

> —**Address, 1963**

It is my belief, for the world in general, that compassion is more important than "religion."

> —**"The True Expression of
> Nonviolence Is Compassion"**

Avalokiteshvara is conceived as the "Lord of Mercy," but the real Avalokiteshvara is compassion itself. In other words, Avalokiteshvara symbolizes an ideal quality most valued by the Tibetans. It is this quality which we must strive to cultivate in ourselves from a limited quantum to the limitless. This undiscriminating, unmotivated, and unlimited compassion for all is obviously not the usual love that you have for your friends, relatives, or family. The love which is limited to your near and dear ones is alloyed with ignorance, with attachment. The kind of love we advocate is the love you can have even for someone who has done harm to you. This kind of love is to be extended to all living beings, and it *can* be extended to all living beings.

—Address, 1973

Compassion is really creating a kind of positive atmosphere, and as a result, you will feel at peace and satisfied. With that kind of mental attitude, naturally wherever there is a compassionate person there is some kind of pleasant atmosphere. One small experience I had many years ago—almost fifty years—was in the summer palace, where I kept some birds, including a small parrot. One of my attendants was an elderly person whose appearance was not very friendly: his eyes were very round and stern, but he was always feeding something to that bird. At the sound of his walking and of some coughing, immediately this small parrot was excited. I wondered about that kind of a response from that small bird, because on the few occasions that I fed him, he never showed that friendly manner. Then I started to use a stick so that the small bird might react differently, but the result was totally negative. Using more force made that poor bird react accordingly—very poorly.

—"Compassion, the Basis for
Human Happiness"

Compassion is, by nature, peaceful and gentle, but it is also very powerful. It is the true sign of inner strength.

—Address, 1992

When we are motivated by wisdom and compassion, the results of our actions benefit everyone, not just our individual selves or some immediate convenience. When we are able to recognize and forgive ignorant actions of the past, we gain the strength to constructively solve the problems of the present.

—"**Thinking Globally: A Universal Task**"

Tolerance and patience with courage are not signs of failure but signs of victory. In your daily life, as you learn more patience, more tolerance with wisdom and courage, you will see it is the true source of success. Actually, if you are too important, that's a real failure.

—**Address, 1984**

Genuine compassion is, as I mentioned before, based on the recognition that others, just like myself, have the right to work on suffering. So, on that basis, even your enemy—same situation, same human being—has the same right. On that basis, you see, you develop a genuine sense of concern: that's compassion. It is unbiased, even toward enemies. So irrespective of what a person's or group of people's attitude is toward you, whether it is hostile or friendly, these people are also sentient beings, human beings, just like myself, and have the right work on suffering: that is genuine compassion.

—"**Compassion, the Basis for
Human Happiness**"

To increase your compassion, visualize yourself, first, as a neutral person. Then on the right side, visualize your old self as a person who is only seeking his or her own welfare, who doesn't think at all about other people, who would take advantage of anyone whenever the chance arises, and who is never content. Visualize your old self that way on the right. Then on the other side of your neutral self, visualize a group of persons who are really suffering and need some help. Now think: All humans have the natural desire to be happy and to avoid suffering; all humans equally have the right to be happy and get rid of suffering. Now you think (wisely, not selfishly) and even if some selfishness must be there, think in a widely selfish way, not in a narrow-minded, selfish way. Everybody wants happiness. Nobody wants foolishness or wants that type of selfish, discontented person.

—Address, 1980

One aspect of that compassion is that you have a sense of caring responsibility. That kind of motivation or that kind of feeling is the one to develop here and extend it to a kind of self-confidence. By increasing confidence you automatically reduce fear, and that will serve as a basis of determination. Success depends on determination, right from the beginning, no matter how difficult the work or the task, no matter how difficult even if one time you fail, a second time you fail, or a third time you fail; it does not matter, if your aim is very clear.

—"Compassion, the Basis for
Human Happiness"

One of the most important things is compassion. We cannot buy it in one of New York City's big shops. We cannot produce it by machine. But by inner development, yes. Without inner peace it is impossible to have world peace.

—Address, 1981

The practice of compassion is not idealistic, but the most effective way to pursue the best interests of others as well as our own. The more we become interdependent, the more it is in our own interest to ensure the well-being of others.

—"Human Rights and Universal Responsibility"

There is no secret. But I thought to myself, our culture is very much based on compassion. We are used to saying all the time, always, "All sentient beings are our fathers and mothers." Even someone who looks like a ruffian or a robber is still someone who has on his mind, "All mothers, all sentient beings." So I myself always practice this thinking.

—Address, 1984

꙳

Compassion is fundamentally a human quality; so its development is not restricted to those who practice religion. Nevertheless, religious traditions have a special role to play in encouraging its development.

—"The True Expression of
Nonviolence Is Compassion"

꙳

Fear arises when we view everyone else with suspicion. It is compassion that creates the sense of trust that allows us to open up to others and reveal our problems, doubts, and uncertainties. Irrespective of whether one is a believer or nonbeliever, as long as we are human beings, as long as we are members of the human family, we need human compassion. So when we have warmth, here, inside, then it brings automatically a sense of responsibility, a sense of commitment. And that brings self-discipline. So therefore, human affection or human compassion is, I feel, one of the very important roots for all good qualities.

—Address, 1995

꙳

Compassion compels us to reach out to all living beings, including our so-called enemies, those people who upset or hurt us. Irrespective of what they do to you, if you remember that all beings like you are only trying to be happy, you will find it much easier to develop compassion toward them.

—"The True Expression of
Nonviolence Is Compassion"

༈

The principles that are set forth in the Theravada scriptures revolve around wisdom, selflessness, and the practice of meditation, which includes the development of the thirty-seven harmonies with enlightenment. These truths have as their basis the good effort of not harming others. Therefore, their basis is compassion.

—**Address, 1981**

༈

I believe that one of the principal factors that hinder us from fully appreciating our interdependence is our undue emphasis on material development. We have become so engrossed in its pursuit that, unknowingly, we have neglected the most basic qualities of compassion, caring, and cooperation. When we do not know someone or do not feel connected to an individual or group, we tend to overlook their needs. Yet the development of human society requires that people help each other.

—**"Human Rights and Universal Responsibility"**

༈

As a Buddhist monk, the cultivation of compassion is an important part of my daily practice. One aspect involves merely sitting quietly in my room, meditating. That can be very good and very comfortable, but the true aim of cultivating compassion is to develop the courage to think of others and to do something for them. For example, as the Dalai Lama I have a responsibility to my people, some of whom are living as refugees and some of whom have remained in Tibet under Chinese occupation. This responsibility means that I have to confront and deal with many problems.

—''The True Expression of
Nonviolence Is Compassion''

✳

Now I think the question is how to obtain compassion. Can we really develop that kind of compassion? My answer is certainly yes. Why? First, this is human nature. Often you see people caught because of human history, in today's situation where basic human nature is aggressive. Now we think, let us remember the time of our conception in our mother's womb and then the time when we were in our mother's womb. The proper child is created through conception taking place in genuine love— that genuine love means respect for each other, not just mad love. Knowing each other really and not just having some love affair, the developing some kind of respect as the basis of a genuine happy marriage. That marriage will remain all of their lives. Starting from that kind of situation, then, according to medical science, an important time for the child is just after birth for a few weeks, during the period that the child's brain is enlarging. During that time, according to medical science, it is the physical touch that is the crucial factor for the proper development of the child's brain. This shows that the physical body needs a mother's affection. Then, after birth the first act from the mother's side is giving milk;

from the child's side the milk is the symbol of compassion without which the child cannot survive. So I think our first act, giving milk, is a symbol of affection.

—"**Compassion, the Basis for Human Happiness**"

Whether one believes in a religion or not, and whether one believes in rebirth or not, there isn't anyone who doesn't appreciate compassion, mercy.

—**Address, 1981**

Determination, with an optimistic attitude, is the key factor for success. Compassion brings us some kind of inner stamp and is developed almost automatically. It opens an inner door, and once through the door we can communicate with other fellow human beings and other sentient beings without much uneasiness. On the other hand, if someone has ill feeling toward others because of their own mental attitude, then other persons also have that kind of feeling. As a result there is suspicion, fear, and automatic distance and difficulties in communicating with others. You feel loneliness, you are isolated due to mental imaginings that all members of the community are looking on you negatively.

—"**Compassion, the Basis for Human Happiness**"

At the heart of Buddhist philosophy is the notion of compassion for others. It should be noted that the compassion encouraged by Mahayana Buddhism is not the usual love one has for friends or family. The love being advocated here is the kind one can have even for another who has done one harm. Developing a kind heart does not always involve any of the sentimental religiosity normally associated with it. It is not just for people who believe in religions; it is for everyone who considers himself or herself to be a member of the human family, and thus sees things in accordingly large terms.

—Address, 1992

Compassion and love are precious things in life. They are not complicated. They are simple, but difficult to practice.

—Address, 1981

We should not think of compassion as being only the preserve of the sacred and religious. It is one of our basic human qualities. Human nature is essentially loving and gentle.

—"The True Expression of
Nonviolence Is Compassion"

Great compassion is the root of all forms of worship.

—Address, 1981

True compassion is universal in scope. It is accompanied by a feeling of responsibility.

—"The True Expression of
Nonviolence Is Compassion"

Who teaches you tolerance? Maybe sometimes your children teach you patience, but always your enemy will teach you tolerance. So your enemy is really your teacher. If you have respect for your enemy instead of anger, your compassion will develop. That type of compassion is real compassion, which is based upon sound beliefs.

—Address, 1980

Humanity

The realization that we are all basically the same human beings, who seek happiness and try to avoid suffering, is very helpful in developing a sense of brotherhood and sisterhood, a warm feeling of love and compassion for others. This, in turn, is essential if we are to survive in this ever shrinking world we live in. For if we each selfishly pursue only what we believe to be in our own interest, without caring about the needs of others, we not only may end up harming others but also ourselves. This fact has become very clear during the course of this century. We know that to wage a nuclear war today, for example, would be a form of suicide; or that by polluting the air or the oceans, in order to achieve some short-term benefit, we are destroying the very basis for our survival.

—Nobel Lecture, 1989

As human brothers and sisters, I have a feeling that deep down we are all the same human beings. Therefore, it is quite natural that when some human brothers and sisters suffer, then other brothers and sisters spontaneously develop some kind of sincere feeling or concern. At this moment I find this very much alive. I consider this a hope for the future.

—Address, 1991

Based on such genuine human relations—real feeling for each other, understanding each other—we can develop mutual trust and respect. From that we can share other people's suffering and build harmony in human society. We can create a friendly human family.

—*Compassion in Global Politics*

If we lose this essential humanity that is our foundation, society as a whole will collapse. What point will there be in pursuing material improvement, and from whom can we demand our rights? Action motivated by compassion and responsibility will ultimately bring good results. Anger and jealousy may be affected in the short term, but will ultimately bring us only trouble.

—"**The True Expression of Nonviolence Is Compassion**"

Under the bright sun, many of us are gathered together with different languages, different styles of dress, perhaps even different faiths. However, all of us are the same in being humans, and we all uniquely have the thought of "I," and we're all the same in wanting happiness and in wanting to avoid suffering.

—**Address, 1984**

I often tell my friends that they have no need to study philosophy, these professional, complicated subjects. Simply just looking at these innocent animals, insects, ants, bees, etc., quite often I develop some kind of respect for them. How? Because they have no religion, no constitution, no police force, nothing. But they live in harmony through the natural law of existence or nature's law or system.

—"**Spirituality and Nature**"

Genuine and true human friends will always share your sorrow, your burdens, and will always come to you whether you are successful or unlucky. So the way to create such a friend is not through anger, not mere education, not mere intelligence, but by the heart—a good heart.

—**Address, 1996**

🌿

Whether people are beautiful and friendly or unattractive and disruptive, ultimately they are human beings. When you recognize that all human beings are equal and like yourself in both their desire for happiness and their right to obtain it, you automatically feel empathy and closeness for them. Through accustoming your mind to this sense of universal altruism, you develop a feeling of responsibility for others: the wish to help them actively overcome their problems. True compassion is not just an emotional response but a firm commitment founded on reason. Therefore, a truly compassionate attitude toward others does not change even if they behave negatively.

—*Disarmament, Peace, and Compassion*

🌿

If you want a genuine friend, we must create a positive atmosphere. After all, we are social animals. I think in our life friends are very important, as are a friendly manner and a genuine smile. How can you find a good smile if you remain stern and suspicious? It is very difficult. Perhaps if you have more power, more money, then I think some people may offer to you an artificial smile, but this is not a very good one. A genuine smile must come from the face of compassion.

—"Compassion, the Basis for
Human Happiness"

🌱

Because we all share this small planet Earth, we have to learn to live in harmony and peace with each other and with nature. That is not just a dream, but a necessity. We are dependent on each other in so many ways that we can no longer live in isolated communities and ignore what is happening outside those communities. We need to help each other when we have difficulties, and we must share the good fortune that we enjoy. I speak to you as just another human being, as a simple monk. If you find what I say useful, then I hope you will try to practice it.

—Nobel Lecture, 1989

🌱

I feel the most important thing is for us to keep in close contact, to express our views frankly, and to make sincere efforts to understand each other. And, through eventual improvement in human relationships, I am confident that our problems can be solved to our mutual satisfaction.

—Address, 1985

🌱

Regardless of race, creed, ideology, political bloc (East and West), or economic region (North and South), the most important and basic aspect of all peoples is their shared humanity—the fact that each person, old, young, rich, poor, educated, uneducated, male or female, is a human. This shared humanness and thus the shared aspiration of gaining happiness and avoiding suffering, as well as the basic right to bring these about, are of prime importance.

—*Spiritual Contributions to Social Progress*

Usually whenever I meet some new person, I feel no need for an introduction, as it is obviously another human being. Maybe in the future, because of technological advances, it may be a robot, but whether it is a robot or a human being, up to now there has been no need for an introduction to something moving, something smiling, something with teeth or eyes. On the physical level we are all the same except color.

—"Compassion, the Basis for
Human Happiness"

When I meet new people in new places, in my mind there is no barrier, no curtain. In my mind, as human beings we are brothers and sisters; there is no difference in substance. I can express whatever I feel, without hesitation, just as to an old friend. With this feeling we can communicate without any difficulty and can contact heart to heart, not with just a few nice words, but really heart to heart.

—*Compassion in Global Politics*

🌱

Egoism is negative; it is very bad. It leads us into trouble. But on the other hand, the strong feeling of "I," of the self, which acts as the basis of determination or will-power, self-confidence; that kind of strong feeling of "I" is very necessary. Without that, how can we develop self-confidence? "No matter how difficult the task, I must do it; I must carry on this work. I will be determined, I am determined to do this." You see, you need the strong sense of "I"; it must be there.

—"Compassion, the Basis for Human Happiness"

🌱

Deep down we must have real affection for each other, a clear realization or recognition of our shared human status. At the same time we must openly accept all ideologies and systems as means of solving humanity's problems. One country, one nation, one ideology, one system, is not sufficient. It is helpful to have a variety of different approaches on the basis of a deep feeling of the basic sameness of humanity. We can then make a joint effort to solve the problems of the whole of humankind. The problems human society is facing in terms of economic development, the crisis of energy, the tensions between the poor and rich nations, and many geopolitical problems can be solved if we understand each other's rights, share each other's problems and sufferings, and then make a joint effort.

—*Compassion in Global Politics*

Religion

There are many religions across the world, with each one promulgating its own message. All religions have "love" and the "spirit of mutual forgiveness" in common. The reality, however, is that differences between religions have resulted in much bloodshed. Confrontations over religion must be stopped.

—**Address, 1995**

From a certain viewpoint religion is a little bit of luxury. If you have religion, very good; even without religion you can survive and you can manage, but without human affection we can't survive. Although anger and hatred, like compassion and love, are part of our mind, still I believe the dominant force of our mind is compassion and human affection. Therefore, usually I call these human qualities spirituality. Not necessarily as a religious message or religion in that sense. Science and technology together with human affection will be constructive. Science and technology under the control of hatred will be destructive.

—**"Spirituality and Nature"**

In our dialogue with rabbis and Jewish scholars, the Tibetan people have learned about the secrets of Jewish spiritual survival in exile. . . . . For two thousand years, even in very difficult times, the Jewish people have remembered their liberation from slavery to freedom, and this has brought you hope in times of difficulty.

—Address, 1997

If we practice religion properly or genuinely, religion is not something outside but in our hearts. The essence of any religion is a good heart. Sometimes I call love and compassion a universal religion. This is my religion. Complicated philosophy, this and that, sometimes creates more trouble and problems. If these sophisticated philosophies are useful for the development of a good heart, then good: use them fully. If these complicated philosophies or systems become an obstacle to a good heart, then it is better to leave them.

—"Spirituality and Nature"

There are many different philosophies. Buddhism, Jainism . . . they do not accept God as a creator. Most other religions, their basic fundamental philosophy is belief in God. There is a big difference. Within these "godless religions," two of the philosophies are based on the theory of independent self, or soul—independent and permanent soul. Buddhists do not accept that. . . . But the basic aim of all these different teachings is serving and helping humanity, trying to create inner peace and, through that, a peaceful human community.

—Address, 1984

It is very useful to strengthen religious belief, religious faith. But in the case where there is no religious faith, then I think here it's important to know whether we should be religious-minded or not. It is an individual right. Without religion we can manage, and in some cases it is even simpler, even better. But you should not forget once you have no more interest about religion; you should not neglect the values of humanity. That's different. As long as we are human beings, as long as we are members of human society, we need human compassion. Without that you can't be a happy human being. Everyone wants a happy life, a successful life, and to be a happy person with a happy family. If you want that, the key factor is human compassion, human affection.

—"Compassion, the Basis for
Human Happiness"

The purpose of religion is not to build beautiful churches or temples, but to cultivate positive human qualities such as tolerance, generosity, and love.

—Address, 1992

You should respect other religions. . . . The essence of all religions is basically the same: to achieve a true sense of brotherhood, a good heart, respect for others. If we can develop these qualities from within our heart, then I think we can actually achieve true peace.

—Address, 1973

Just as when we fight external suffering, we have to undergo suffering, and so forth, so when we undergo any
strife internally, there is indeed internal pain. Therefore,
religion is something internal to be thought about.

—**Address, 1983**

Every world religion, no matter what its philosophical
view, is founded first and foremost on the precept that we
must reduce our selfishness and serve others. Unfortunately, sometimes in the name of religion, people cause
more quarrels than they solve. Practitioners of different
faiths should realize that each religious tradition has immense intrinsic value as a means for providing mental
and spiritual health.

—**"Universal Responsibility and
Our Global Environment"**

Without accepting a religion, but simply developing a realization of the importance of compassion and love, and
with more concern and respect for others, a kind of spiritual development is very possible for those persons who
are outside of religion.

—**Address, 1985**

Whether one accepts religion or not is a person's individual right. But one thing I feel is that when people lose

interest toward religion, they also neglect the deeper human values. I think that is a problem. Now, therefore, we have to find ways and means to increase the deeper human values such as a secular ethic. So here I believe that educational institutions have the key road. Religious institutions, of course, have the great responsibility, but their responsibility is limited. But educational institutions, everywhere, now become important . . . in every way, to improve basic human good quality.

—Address, 1995

The Christians and Buddhists have basically the same teaching, the same aim. The world now becomes smaller and smaller and smaller, due to good communications and other factors also. With that development, different faiths and different cultures also come closer and closer. This is, I think, very good. If we understand each other's way of living, thinking, different philosophies, and different faiths, it can contribute to mutual understanding. By understanding each other, naturally we will develop true harmony and the ability to make joint efforts. And I always feel that this special inner development is something very important for mankind.

—Address, 1983

The common factor among all religions is that, whatever the philosophical differences between them, they are primarily concerned with helping their followers become better human beings. Consequently, all religions encourage the practice of kindness, generosity, and concern for others.

—''**The True Expression of Nonviolence Is Compassion**''

🌻

We need to clearly recognize that the basic aim of all religions is the same. Since all religions are for the sake of taming our minds to make us better persons, we need to bring all religious practice into a healing of our minds. It's not at all good, and extremely unfortunate, to use the doctrines and practices that are for the sake of taming the mind as reasons for becoming biased. Therefore it is extremely important for us to be nonsectarian. As Buddhists, we need to respect the Christians, the Jews, the Hindus, and so on.

—**Address, 1986**

🌻

Every religion of the world has similar ideals of love, the same goal of benefiting humanity through spiritual practice, and the same effect of making their followers into better human beings. The common goal of all moral precepts laid down by the great teachers of humanity is unselfishness. All religions agree upon the necessity to control the undisciplined mind that harbors selfishness and other roots of trouble. And each, in its own way, teaches a path leading to a spiritual state that is peaceful, disciplined, ethical, and wise, thus helping living beings to avoid misery and gain happiness. It is for these reasons that I have always believed all religions, essentially, have the same message.

—Address, 1981

Each of us in our own way can try to spread compassion into people's hearts. Western civilizations these days place great importance on filling the human "brain" with knowledge, but no one seems to care about filling the human "heart" with compassion. This is what the real role of religion is.

—Address, 1995

All religions agree upon the necessity to control the un-disciplined mind that harbors selfishness and other roots of trouble, and each teaches a path leading to a spiritual state that is peaceful, disciplined, ethical, and wise. It is in this sense that I believe all religions have essentially the same message. Differences of dogma may be ascribed to differences of time and circumstances as well as cultural influences; indeed, there is no end to scholastic argument when we consider the purely metaphysical side of reli-gion. However, it is much more beneficial to try to imple-ment daily the shared precepts for goodness taught by all religions rather than to argue about minor differences in approach.

—*Compassion in Global Politics*

🌿

Just as each religion has its own respective philosophy and there are similarities as well as differences among the various religions, so we must go according to what is suitable to each individual. Just as in the world you have many different kinds of food—for example, on my present tour of European countries I have had quite a variety—so there are many different kinds of dishes. You cannot tell all the people that they must take one particular kind of food. What is important is what is suitable for a particular person. For example, in the different good habits of different people we don't have any disputes, because each one takes what is suitable for him. Similarly religion is a food for the mind, and as we all have different tastes, we must take that which is most suitable for us.

—Address, 1973

🌿

I maintain that every major religion of the world— Buddhism, Christianity, Confucianism, Hinduism, Islam, Jainism, Sikhism, Taoism, Zoroastrianism—has similar ideals of love, the same goal of benefiting humanity through spiritual practice, and the same effect of making their followers into better human beings. All religions teach moral precepts for perfecting the functions of mind, body, and speech. All teach us not to lie or steal or take others' lives and so on. The common goal of all moral precepts laid down by the great teachers of humanity is unselfishness. The great teachers wanted to lead their followers away from the paths of negative deeds caused by ignorance and to introduce them to paths of goodness.

—**Address, 1986**

There should be a balance between material and spiritual progress, a balance achieved through the principles based on love and compassion. Love and compassion are the essence of all religion.

—**Address, 1984**

All major religions are basically the same in that they emphasize peace of mind and kindness, but it is very important to practice this in our daily lives, not just in a church or a temple.

—**Address, 1987**

Leaders of each religion should become better acquainted with one another and should exchange information on their respective traditions. I have visited many holy sites around the world, including Jerusalem, and though I am a Buddhist who does not believe in God, these were very profound experiences for me. Such visits will enable us to enhance our mutual understanding, and are necessary to promote religious harmony.

—**Address, 1995**

The population of our planet is over five billion. Of these perhaps one billion actively and sincerely follow a formal religion. The remaining over four billion are not believers in the true sense. If we regard the development of compassion and other good qualities as the business only of religion, these over four billion, the majority, will be excluded. As brothers and sisters, members of our great human family, every one of these people has the potential to be inspired by the need for compassion, can be developed and nurtured without following or practicing a particular religion.

—"The True Expression of
Nonviolence Is Compassion"

When we became refugees, we knew our struggle would not be easy; it would take a long time, generations. Very often we would refer to the Jewish people, how they kept their identity and faith despite such hardship and so much suffering. And when external conditions were ripe, they were ready to rebuild their nation. So you see, there are many things to learn from our Jewish brothers and sisters.

—Address, 1997

I don't think religious teaching is easy to wipe out, but very difficult. Once it is deep-rooted, I don't think it is easy to destroy. The actual threat comes from the inside.

That means you see, those so-called "religious persons" who do not practice well, do not follow a proper way. That is the most dangerous, the greatest threat.

—Address, 1985

Religion can and should be used by any people or person who finds it beneficial. What is important for each seeker is to choose the religion which is most suitable to himself. However, I believe that the embracing of a particular religion like Buddhism does not mean the rejection of another religion or one's own community. In fact, it is important that those of you who have embraced Buddhism should not cut yourselves off from your own society; you should continue to live within your own community and with its members.

—Address, 1973

Buddhists can't make the whole world population become Buddhist. That's impossible. Christians cannot convert all mankind to Christianity. And Hindus cannot govern all mankind. Over the past many centuries, if you look unbiasedly, each faith, each great teaching, has served mankind very much. So it's much better to make friends and understand each other and make an effort to serve humankind rather than criticize or argue. This is my belief.

—Address, 1981

In ancient times, when communities were isolated, it was fine to believe that one's religion was the only true religion. But these days, when society is more diversified and national borders have less meaning, the idea of religious pluralism is more beneficial.

—Address, 1995

If I say that all religions and philosophies are the same, that is hypocritical, not true. There are differences. I believe there's a hundred percent possibility to make real peace and to help shoulder to shoulder and serve humankind. Equally, we have no responsibility and no right to impose on a nonbeliever.

—Address, 1981

The real objective of religion is to serve the functions of a protector—a source of refuge. A system which provides security makes a utilitarian, functional religion. And yet whatever and howsoever might be the external activities, behavior, and forms provided for by the system, it cannot be viewed as falling within the perspective of a functional religion if it fails to provide, even elementarily, a means of refuge or protection.

—Address, 1973

I think it's helpful to have many different religions, since our human mind always likes different approaches for different dispositions. Just like food. There are some people who prefer bread and some who prefer rice and some who prefer flour. Each has different tastes, and each eats food that accords with his own taste. Some eat rice, some eat flour, but there is no quarrel. Nobody says, "Oh, you are eating rice." In the same way, there is mental variety. So for certain people the Christian religion is more useful, more applicable. It's a basic belief. Some people say, "There's a God, there's a Creator, and everything depends on His acts, so you should be impressed because with that security, with more belief, you will prefer that approach. Other people say that with our Buddhist belief there is no creator and that everything depends on you, you should be impressed—that is preferable.

—Address, 1981

For a truly religious person there is never any basis for quarrel or dispute. Yet it is a fact there have been so-called religious wars. However, the people involved in these were not practicing religion but were merely using religion as an instrument of power. The actual motivation was selfish, not spiritual. Religious wars are not a question of contradictions between religions at all.

—Address, 1973

In Tibet there used to be a few Tibetan Christians. They followed the Christian faith but remained very much Tibetan. There is a verse by an ancient Tibetan which says that you must change your mind but your external behavior should remain as it is.

—Address, 1973

Death and Liberation

A king loses his kingdom, and a crippled beggar leaves behind his walking stick. We should quickly seize enlightenment while we still have the chance. In much less than a century all of us will be dead. Maybe someone will say, "The Dalai Lama once gave a sermon here"; only this faint memory of today will remain. We cannot be sure that we will be alive even tomorrow. There is no time to procrastinate. I who am giving this teaching have no guarantee that I will live out this day.

—*The Buddhist Approach to Knowledge*

Once one understands the nature of cyclic existence . . . . one can be free of it.

—Address, 1980

We must take direct responsibility for our own spiritual lives and rely upon nobody and nothing, for even the Buddhas of the ten directions and three times are unable to help us if we do not help ourselves. If another being were able to save us, surely he would already have done so. It is time, therefore, that we help ourselves.

The Buddhist Approach to Knowledge

When I am alive, I should utilize my energy, my existence, for good, for the benefit of others. That's important. Then I'm finished. Whether people say good things or bad things doesn't matter. . . . When I reach Nirvana, then I will tell everything!

—Address, 1996

At the moment we are blessed with human life and with all the possibilities that this implies. Unlike animals and lower life forms, we are able to pluck the fruit of enlightenment, an act of ultimate goodness to both ourselves and others. However, death is pressing upon us from every side, threatening to rob us of this precious opportunity at any moment, and when we die nothing can be taken with us but the seeds of our life's work and our spiritual knowledge.

—*The Buddhist Approach to Knowledge*

Even if we cannot solve certain problems, we should not regret it. We humans must face death, old age, and disease as well as natural disasters, such as hurricanes, that are beyond our control. We must face them; we cannot avoid them. But these sufferings are quite sufficient for us—why should we create other problems due to our own ideology, just differing ways of thinking? Useless! It is sad. Thousands upon thousands of people suffer from this. Such a situation is truly silly since we can avoid it by adopting a different attitude, appreciating the basic humanity which ideologies are supposed to serve.

—*Address, 1982*

All compounded things are subject to disintegration. Since experience and knowledge are impermanent and subject to disintegration, the mind of which they are functions is not something that remains constant and eternal. From moment to moment it undergoes change and disintegration.

—*Happiness, Karma, and the Mind*

The human body as a configuration of energy is made up of seventy-two thousand channels, the currents of energy which travel through them, and the essential drops or units of consciousness and energy conjoined which reside in the channels. By manipulating the essential drops within the channels by way of the currents, we undergo different levels or states of consciousness. The type of consciousness we now have based on our present configuration is one type, dream another, deep sleep another. Fainting, heavy fainting or coma or when breath stops are all others. The final level of consciousness, Clear Light, is made manifest at the time of death. This is the strongest and subtlest. Unused, it serves as the basis for revolving the round of birth, old age, sickness, and death.

—Address, 1980

If we use this human brain for something of little import, that is very sad. If we spend our time just concerned with the affairs of this lifetime up to the point of death, that is very sad and weak. We need to decide that it is completely perverse. When we think in this manner, the emphasis just on this lifetime becomes weaker and weaker. It is said that we should renounce this life. That doesn't mean that we should go hungry or not take care of this lifetime at all, but that we should reduce our attachment to affairs that are limited to this lifetime. Now, when we reduce the emphasis on the appearances of this lifetime and the appearances of future lifetimes come to the mind, it is necessary to investigate those also. Because in the future, even though one attains a good lifetime, there will be a lifetime after that lifetime, and a lifetime after that lifetime.

—Address, 1982

During one of my interviews with German television, one
written question put to me was that Westerners very
much fear death and Easterners don't fear death. Why is
it? Then I told the interviewer that I believed the contrary.
You Westerners love war, you love these horrible weapons. These weapons kill, and war means death, and it is
not natural death. This is awful and it seems you have no
fear of death! We Tibetans, in our time, saw soldiers and
the military as something negative. That means we have
more fear of death!

—**"Universal Responsibility and the
Inner Environment"**

I am a Buddhist. I believe that a human being may take
on the form of a lower being. Where you are born in the
next life is not dependent on your present body. This is
dependent on unwholesome activities and virtue. The
basic thing is our own karmic force. That is the seed. The
seed alone, however, is not sufficient—it must interact
with water and soil. So similarly you have to think not
only in terms of cause but also in terms of conditions.
Basically it is very clear. The main material of our physical body comes from parents. But our mind, our self, does
not.

—**Address, 1984**

In the search for ultimate truth, if it fails to dawn on us,
it is we who have not found it. Ultimate truth exists. If

we think deeply and reflect carefully, we shall realize that we ourselves have our existence in ultimate truth. For example, I am talking to you and you are listening to me. We are generally under the impression that there is a speaker and an audience, that there is the sound of words being spoken, but in ultimate death, if I search for myself I will not find it, and if you search for yourselves you will not find them. Neither speaker nor audience, neither words nor sound, can be found.

—*The Two Truths*

Bodhimind forms the central theme of Mahayana Buddhism in Tibet. We believe that the concept of the Bodhimind will go a long way in helping to achieve basic unity and a spirit of cooperation among the followers of different creeds. . . . The inspiration to achieve this ineffable Bodhimind can be expressed this way: "I must attain the supreme state of omniscient Buddhahood so that I can liberate all sentient beings from their ocean of misery, Samsara, and establish them in the ultimate happiness of Nirvana." This inspiration creates a longing to devote one's energy to both the profound and extensive stages of the path of Mahayana. It is the root of the practice for accomplishing the Bodhisattva deeds, which connotes generosity, morality, patience, perseverance, meditation, and wisdom.

—*Love and Compassion*

Liberation or salvation means freedom from bondage. Beings are ensnared and bound by karma and delusion. When the unsatisfactoriness or *dukkha* resulting from the bondage of . . . karma and delusion, or the state of unsatisfactoriness experienced owing to related influences of karma and delusion, is eradicated and tranquilized, one dwells in the state known as liberation. It is true that the various schools of Buddhist thought differ in expounding the true nature and import of the term *liberation*. However, broadly speaking, it can be interpreted as the destruction of or freedom from unsatisfactoriness and its causes, given rise to by one's karma and delusion and their resulting dominant influences.

—**Address, 1979**

As Buddhists, we all believe in the law of karma, the natural law of cause and effect. Whatever external causal conditions someone comes across in subsequent lives result from the accumulation of that individual's actions in previous lives. When the karmic force of past deeds reaches maturity, a person experiences pleasurable and unpleasurable mental states. They are but a natural consequence of his own previous actions.

—*Happiness, Karma, and the Mind*

It is in dependence upon sentient beings that one first generates this altruistic aspiration to highest Enlightenment, and it is in relation to sentient beings that one practices the deeds of the path in order to achieve enlightenment, and it is for the sake of sentient beings that one achieves Buddhahood. Therefore, sentient beings are the object of observation, the basis of all this marvelous development. Therefore, they are more important than even the wish-granting jewel, and one should treat them respectfully and kindly.

—**Address, 1981**

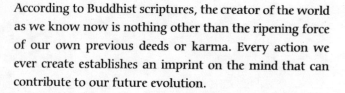

According to Buddhist scriptures, the creator of the world as we know now is nothing other than the ripening force of our own previous deeds or karma. Every action we ever create establishes an imprint on the mind that can contribute to our future evolution.

—*The Buddhist Approach to Knowledge*

As long as you are a human being, a member of the human family, you need others' warm feeling, and therefore it is most important that you try to get more warm feeling, be warm-hearted. . . . If someone lives with these qualities, even an extreme atheist, the Buddhist viewpoint is that when life ends, if a person has lived within this life very honestly and as a good person, then because of that behavior he will get a good result in the next life. On the contrary, one who has talked about the future life and

Nirvana very much without that practice, although that person belonged to the category of spiritual groups, in reality he will face more problems.

—**Address, 1985**

Section Two

THE WORLD AND TIBET

The Sheltering Tree of Interdependence

O Lord Tathagata
Born of the Iksvkus tree
Peerless One
Who, seeing the all-pervasive nature
Of interdependence
Between the environment and sentient beings
Samsara and Nirvana
Moving and unmoving
Teaches the world out of compassion
Bestow thy benevolence on us

O the Savior
The One called Avalokiteshvara
Personifying the body of compassion
Of all Buddhas
We beseech thee to make our spirits open
And fructify to observe reality
Bereft of illusion

Our obdurate egocentricity
Ingrained in our minds
Since beginningless time
Contaminates, defiles, and pollutes
The environment
Created by the common karma
Of all sentient beings

Lakes and ponds have lost
Their clarity, their coolness
The atmosphere is poisoned
Nature's celestial canopy in the fiery firmament
Has burst asunder
And sentient beings suffer diseases
Unknown before

Perennial snow mountains resplendent in their glory
Bow down and melt into water
The majestic oceans lose their ageless equilibrium
And inundate islands

The dangers of fire, water, and wind are limitless
Sweltering heat dries up our lush forests
Lashing our world with unprecedented storms
And the oceans surrender their salt to the elements

Though people lack not wealth
They cannot afford to breathe clean air
Rains and streams cleanse not
But remain inert and powerless liquids

Human beings
And countless beings
That inhabit water and land
Reel under the yoke of physical pain
Caused by malevolent diseases
Their minds are dulled
With sloth, stupor, and ignorance
The joys of the body and spirit
Are far, far away

We needlessly pollute
The fair bosom of our mother earth
Rip out her trees to feed our short-sighted greed
Turning our fertile earth into a sterile desert

The interdependent nature
Of the external environment
And people's inward nature
Described in Tantras

Works on medicine and astronomy
Has verily been vindicated
By our present experience

The earth is home to living beings;
Equal and impartial to the moving and unmoving
Thus spoke the Buddha in truthful voice
With the great earth for witness

As a noble being recognizes the kindness
Of a sentient mother
And makes recompense for it
So the earth, the universal mother,
Which nurtures all equally,
Should be regarded with affection and care

Forsake wastage
Pollute not the clean, clear nature
Of the four elements
And destroy the well-being of people
But absorb yourself in actions
That are beneficial to all

Under a tree was the great Sage Buddha born
Under a tree, he overcame passion
And attained enlightenment
Under two trees did he pass in Nirvana
Verily, the Buddha held the tree in great esteem

Here, where Mañjusri's emanation
Lama Tson Khapa's body bloomed forth
Is marked by a sandal tree
Bearing a hundred thousand images of the Buddha

Is it not well known
That some transcendental deities
Eminent local deities and spirits
Make their abode in trees?

Flourishing trees clean the wind
Help us breathe the sustaining air of life
They please the eye and soothe the mind
Their shade makes welcome resting place

In Vinaya, the Buddha taught monks
To care for tender trees
From this we learn the virtue
Of planting, of nurturing trees

The Buddha forbade monks to cut
Cause others to cut living plants
Destroy seeds or defile the fresh green grass
Should this not inspire us
To love and protect our environment?

They say, in the celestial realms
The trees emanate
The Buddha's blessings
And echo the sound
Of basic Buddhist doctrines
Like impermanence

It is trees that bring rain
Trees that hold the essence of the soil
Kalpa-Taru, the tree of wish fulfillment
Virtually resides on earth
To serve all purposes

In times of yore
Our forebears ate the fruits of trees
Wore their leaves

Discovered fire by the attrition of wood
Took refuge amidst the foliage of trees
When they encountered danger

Even in this age of science
Of technology
Trees provide us shelter
The chairs we sit in
The beds we lie on
When the heart is ablaze
With the fire of anger
Fueled by wrangling
Trees bring refreshing, welcome coolness

In the trees lie the roots
Of all life on earth
When it vanishes
The land exemplified by the name
Of the Jambu tree
Will remain no more
Than a dreary, desolate desert

Nothing is dearer to the living than life
Recognizing this, in the Vinaya rules
The Buddha lays down prohibitions
Like the use of water with living creatures

In the remoteness of the Himalayas
In the days of yore, the land of Tibet
Observed a ban on hunting, on fishing
And, during designated periods, even construction
These traditions are noble
For they preserve and cherish
The lives of humble, helpless, defenseless creatures

Playing with the lives of other beings
Without sensitivity or hesitation
As in the act of hunting or fishing for sport
Is an act of heedless, needless violence
A violation of the solemn rights
Of all living beings

Being attentive to the nature
Of interdependence of all creatures
Both animate and inanimate

One should never slacken in one's efforts
To preserve and conserve nature's energy

On a certain day, month, and year
One should observe the ceremony
Of tree planting

Thus, one fulfills one's responsibilities
Serves one's fellow beings
Which not only brings one's happiness
But benefits all

May the force of observing that which is right
And abstinence from wrong practices and evil deeds
Nourish and augment the prosperity of the world
May it invigorate living beings and help them blossom
May sylvan joy and pristine happiness
Ever increase, ever spread and encompass all that is

—The Sheltering Tree of
Interdependence: A Buddhist Monk's Reflections
on Ecological Responsibility

Tibet

Tibet, known to many as the Roof of the World, is a land which abounds in great natural beauty and clean, pure air. It is a haven for those who wish to escape the tense, unhealthy surroundings often caused by modern "progress." For centuries we Tibetans have lived in peace and harmony with our environment, in accordance with Buddhist tenets of love and compassion and by an admirable code of ethics and civility.

—*The True Face of Tibet*

Tibet—an ancient nation with a unique culture and civilization—is disappearing fast. In endeavoring to protect my nation from this catastrophe, I have always sought to be guided by realism, moderation, and patience. I have tried in every way I know to find some mutually acceptable solution in the spirit of reconciliation and compromise. However, it has now become clear that our efforts alone are not sufficient to bring the Chinese government to the negotiating table. I am, therefore, left with no other choice but to appeal to the international community for urgent intervention and action on behalf of my people.

—**Address, 1996**

I propose that the whole of Tibet, including the eastern provinces of Kham and Amdo, be transformed into a zone of "Ahimsa," a Hindi term used to mean a state of peace and nonviolence. The establishment of such a peace zone would be in keeping with Tibet's historical role as a peaceful and neutral Buddhist nation and buffer state separating the continent's great powers. It would also be in keeping with Nepal's proposal to proclaim Nepal a peace zone and with China's declared support for such a proclamation. The peace zone proposed by Nepal would have a much greater impact if it was to include Tibet and neighboring areas.

—**Five Point Peace Plan**

What happens in Tibet is also important from a strategic point of view, because regional peace and stability are tied to the solution of the Tibet question.

—**Address, 1995**

I think it is important that we as Tibetans present a clear and factual account of the Tibetan situation. This is particularly necessary now when the present Chinese leadership is reported to be following a moderate and responsible path. It remains to be seen whether Chinese leaders are prepared to recognize realities as they really exist, or whether they will continue to direct facts in order to draw conclusions that serve only China's interests.

—**"China and the Future of Tibet"**

Irrespective of what is its political status, one of my main aims is [that] Tibet should be demilitarized, should be a zone of peace.

—**Address, 1995**

Demilitarization will free great human resources for protection of the environment, relief of poverty, and sustainable human development. It is my hope that the United States can soon help make this a reality. I have always envisioned the future of my own country, Tibet, to be founded on this basis. Tibet would be a neutral, demilitarized sanctuary where weapons are forbidden and the people live in harmony with nature. This is not merely a dream—it is precisely the way Tibetans tried to live for over a thousand years before our country was tragically invaded.

—"Universal Responsibility and
Our Global Environment"

There appears to be an erroneous impression amongst many people that the problem of Tibet is the institution of the Dalai Lama. What I understand is the problem is not with the institution of the Dalai Lama but that the problem is about views and beliefs of six million Tibetans. . . . For myself, I am a simple monk. I am not particularly concerned with the institution of the Dalai Lama, but ultimately it is for the people to decide.

—Address, 1984

Tibet is distinguished by its extraordinary geography, the unique race and language of its people, and the rich culture they have developed over 2,100 years of recorded history. Approximately six million Tibetans populate our country, which covers around 2.5 million square kilometers, an area the size of Western Europe.

—*The True Face of Tibet*

🦎✽

We are not against China; we have no ill feelings toward our Chinese brothers and sisters. Even to those individual Chinese who make decisions of brutality on the spot, as a Buddhist practitioner we have more concern about these people, more compassion to the people who create pain and suffering on others than on the victims, for whom there is some reason to feel concern. The victims are already ripening as a result of their negative karma, but the person who creates pain on others, that is the start of a new karma and long-term consequences will have to be faced.

—''**The Need to Balance Spiritual and Material Values**''

🦎✽

In the future I envision Tibet as an anchor of peace and stability at the heart of Asia: a zone of nonviolence where humanity and nature live in harmony. For hundreds of years the Tibetan plateau was a vital buffer between Asia's great powers: Russia, China, and India. Until Tibet is once more demilitarized and restored to its historical neutrality, there can be no firm foundation for peace in Asia. The first step is to recognize the truth of my country's status, that of a nation under foreign occupation.

—**Address, 1991**

༝

The issue isn't whether the Dalai Lama and the one hundred thousand refugees would be able to return to Tibet. The reason we appeal to other nations isn't because we want to go back and the Chinese aren't allowing us in. It isn't that I long for some of the privileges I used to enjoy and am bitter with the Chinese for having reduced me to the status of a refugee. . . . The real issues are the feelings and welfare of the six million Tibetans still left in Tibet. Why should an alien rule be forced upon them? Why shouldn't they have the choice of holding their own beliefs, traditions, culture, and identity?

—*Misconceptions and Realities*
of the Tibetan Issue

༝

For centuries the Tibetan and Chinese peoples have lived as neighbors—friendly for most of the period, but occasionally at war and in confrontation with each other. In the future, also, we have no other alternative but to live as neighbors. Therefore, I have always encouraged Tibetans in exile to meet with Chinese people, to make friends with them and develop personal relationships with them. I make it a point to ask the Tibetans to understand the distinction between the Chinese people and Chinese goverment policy.

—*Address, 1995*

༝

If each and every Tibetan makes an effort and works for the common cause, it will not be long before the sun of happiness shines on Tibet. When the joyful occasion of the reunion of Tibetans in Tibet and those in exile comes about, Tibet—with all its three provinces—will follow a genuine path of freedom, democracy, and unity based on the wishes of the people. As the Guidelines for Future Tibet's Policy and Basic Features of its Constitution stipulates, Tibetan democracy will be based on the Buddhist principles of compassion, justice, and equality. Tibet will become a zone of peace with environmental protection as one of the guiding principles of its government.

—**Message on World Human Rights Day, 1993**

I consider my commitment to Tibetan freedom status is part of spiritual practice. Unless some degree of freedom or autonomy materializes, sooner or later Tibetan Buddhist culture will die.

—**Address, 1997**

Fundamentally, the issue of Tibet is political. It is an issue of colonial rule: the oppression of Tibet by the People's Republic of China and resistance to that rule by the people of Tibet. This issue can be resolved only through negotiations and not, as China would have it, through force, intimidation, and population transfer.

—**Address, 1996**

I believe that Tibet will be free only when its people become strong, and hatred is not strength. It is a weakness.

The Lord Buddha was not being religious, in the popular sense of the term, when He said that hatred does not cease by hatred. Rather, he was being practical. Any achievement attained through hatred can neither be lasting nor binding. It would only be inviting trouble sooner or later.

—Statement, March 10, 1971

In my efforts to seek a negotiated solution to our problem, I have refrained from asking for the complete independence of Tibet. Historically and according to international law Tibet is an independent country under Chinese occupation. However, over the past fifteen years I have adopted a middle-way approach of reconciliation and compromise in the pursuit of a peaceful and negotiated resolution of the Tibetan issue. While it is the overwhelming desire of the Tibetan people to regain their national independence, I have repeatedly and publicly stated that I am willing to enter into negotiations on the basis of an agenda that does not include the independence. The continued occupation of Tibet poses an increasing threat to the very existence of a distinct Tibetan national and cultural identity. Therefore, I consider that my primary responsibility is to take whatever steps I must to save my people and their unique heritage from total annihilation.

—Address, 1995

I really feel that Buddhist culture—which today is facing the threat of extinction—must be saved. How to save it?

Through dialogue. For dialogue, my own effort for the last now more than sixteen years has not brought satisfactory results. Therefore, there's no other choice except to appeal to the international community.

—"**The Need to Balance Spiritual and Material Values**"

You see, a nation is dying. My strength comes from the justice of my cause, and I think from my compassion, but I need help. Not just with a few nice words, but with some kind of action. I believe that usually young people are very good at action.

—**Address, 1996**

In Europe, where the tectonic plates of Christianity, Islam, and Orthodox religions meet in the Balkans, there has been recurring and tragic conflict. Tibet occupies a similar place in Asia, surrounded by Hinduism, Islam, and Buddhism. And yet Tibet, because of the peaceful way of its people, has been able to remain stable and prevent direct confrontation between these groups. I have therefore called for Tibet to be turned into a zone of Ahimsa, a zone of peace. Such demilitarized zones have been created in other parts of the world. Doing so in Tibet would also allow us to play our historical role in maintaining peace in Central and South Asia.

—**Address, 1995**

᧗

In the majestic beauty of Tibet's natural surroundings, the people developed their culture, which was deeply influenced by the Buddhist teachings of India. Though materially backward, Tibetan society was highly sophisticated in terms of mental and spiritual development. This brought about peace and harmony in the minds of our people and our communities. The faces of Tibetans who grew up and lived in this environment of the past immediately reveal the natural calmness and spontaneity which is so frequently commented upon by visitors from around the world.

—The True Face of Tibet

᧗

In spite of the very serious, harsh, repressive nature of what is happening in Tibet today, basically, I am very hopeful, because the overall situation in the world is that the totalitarian communist way of ruling does not work. And then in China the democratic movement not only survived, but is now very active.

—Address, 1995

᧗

In the past I have deliberately restrained myself from emphasizing the historical and legal status of Tibet. It is my belief that it is more important to look forward to the future than dwell in the past. Theoretically speaking, it is not impossible that the six million Tibetans could benefit from joining one billion Chinese of their own free will, if a relationship based on equity, mutual benefit, and mutual respect could be established. If China wants Tibet to stay with China, then she must create the necessary conditions. However, the reality today is that Tibet is an occupied country under colonial rule. This is the essential issue which must be addressed and resolved through negotiations.

—**Address, 1996**

🦎

It is easier to feel concern about these people and about the Tibetan Buddhist culture, essentially a culture of peace and of nonviolence. Its survival, which is at the moment facing extinction, not only benefits six million Tibetan people, but also millions of people sharing the same Buddhist culture, the whole of the modern Himalayas and Mongolia, Mongols not only in Mongolia or China but also in the Russian Federation, and furthermore millions of young Chinese who share a Tibetan Buddhist culture.

—**"The Need to Balance Spiritual
and Material Values"**

🦎

Unfortunately, the Chinese government's response to these proposals has been one of total rejection. I am referred to as a "splittist" who is trying to internationalize the Tibet issue. In fact, what I have been trying to do is merely to preserve Tibet's cultural and national identity and to find a fair solution to our problem, one which is mutually acceptable and beneficial to both Tibet and China.

—Address, 1995

In the final analysis it is for the Tibetan and the Chinese peoples themselves to find a just and peaceful resolution to the Tibetan problem. Therefore, in our struggle for freedom and justice I have always tried to pursue a path of nonviolence in order to ensure that a relationship based on mutual respect, friendship, and genuine good neighborliness can be sustained between our two peoples in the future.

—Address, 1996

The tragedy of Tibet is that a whole race, a people strongly opposed to foreign domination, has been subjugated, oppressed, and gobbled up by China. This has happened not only to Tibet but also to Mongolia and Eastern Turkestan. . . . It may not sound right for me to speak of these two other countries, which are in a similar situation, but I happen to know the true feelings and the national aspirations of these people. Their feelings of resentment against Chinese domination are no less than those of the Tibetans.

—*Misconceptions and Realities*
of the Tibetan Issue

The Tibetan struggle is a struggle for survival—for the survival of a people, a civilization, a unique culture and spiritual tradition, and for our environment.

—Address, 1995

Tibet had been an independent country for over a thousand years, and I believe that the Tibetan people do have the right to choose independence. However, it is also a political reality that Tibet is now under Chinese rule. Therefore, in order to find a mutually acceptable solution, I have tried a "middle-way" approach to solve the problem. My approach is also in response to Mr. Deng Xiaoping's message that "anything except independence can be discussed." Accordingly, over the last fifteen years six official delegations were sent to China and Tibet, and my personal envoy visited China at least ten times. I also made several proposals to the Chinese government. These proposals were announced at prestigious international forums to show my seriousness and sincerity.

—Address, 1995

The present Chinese leaders should give up the past dogmatic narrow-mindedness and fear of losing face and recognize the present world situations. They should accept their mistakes, the realities, and the right of all peoples of the human race to equality and happiness. Acceptance of this should not be merely on paper; it should be put into practice. If these are accepted and strictly followed, all problems can be solved with honesty and justice.

—Statement, March 10, 1979

※

As the Dalai Lama, my main concern is Tibet and six million of the country's people. As a Buddhist monk, I have to try to be concerned with means to contribute to the welfare of all beings—even insects and animals—and particularly, humanity. Third, as a human being, I always feel that today we need the realization of oneness of all human beings.

—Address, 1986

※

The Tibet issue will neither go away of its own accord, nor can it be wished away. As the past has clearly shown, neither intimidation nor coercion of the Tibetan people can force a solution. Sooner or later the leadership in Beijing will have to face this fact. Actually, the Tibet problem represents an opportunity for China. If it was solved properly through negotiation, not only would it be helpful in creating a political atmosphere conducive to the smooth transition of China into a new era, but also China's image throughout the world would be greatly enhanced. A properly negotiated settlement would furthermore have a strong positive impact on the peoples of both Hong Kong and Taiwan and will do much to improve Sino-Indian relations by inspiring genuine trust and confidence. Moreover, if our Buddhist culture can flourish once again in Tibet, we are confident of being able to make a significant contribution to millions of our Chinese brothers and sisters by sharing with them those spiritual and moral values which are so clearly lacking in China today.

—Address, 1996

I am still committed to the spirit of my "Middle Way" approach, and I am hopeful that continued international efforts to persuade the Chinese government to enter into negotiations with us may eventually yield tangible results.

—Statement, March 10, 1995

Today, when the world is entering the twenty-first century, China is also at a critical conjunction. It is rapidly becoming an economic as well as a political and military power. At the same time, Chinese society is undergoing profound changes. The Chinese leadership is facing a generational change. Freedom, democracy, equality, human rights, will sooner or later be demanded by its people. A transformation from the current totalitarian regime into a more open, democratic one is inevitable; the only question is how and when, and whether it will be a smooth transition or a hard one.

—Address, 1995

I am considering the possibility of a visit to Tibet as early as possible. I have in mind two purposes for such a visit. First, I want to ascertain the situation in Tibet myself on the spot and communicate directly with my people. By doing so I also hope to help the Chinese leadership to understand the true feelings of Tibetans. It would be important, therefore, for senior Chinese leaders to accompany me on such a visit, and that outside observers, including the press, be present to see and report their findings. Second, I wish to advise and persuade my people not to abandon nonviolence as the appropriate form of struggle. My ability to talk to my own people can be a key factor in bringing about a peaceful solution. My visit could be a new opportunity to promote understanding and create a basis for a negotiated solution.

—Address, 1991

Democracy in China will have important consequences for Tibet. Many of the leaders of the Chinese democracy movement recognize that Tibetans have been ill-treated by Beijing and believe that such injustice should be redressed. Many of them openly state that Tibetans should be granted the opportunity to express and implement their right to self-determination. Even under the present one-party rule China has undergone dramatic changes in the last fifteen, sixteen years. These changes will continue. I remain optimistic that this transformation will make it possible for the Chinese leaders and encourage them to resolve the problem of Tibet peacefully through dialogue.

—Address, 1996

We must improve the relationship between China and Tibet as well as between Tibetans in and outside Tibet. With truth and equality as our foundation, we must try to develop friendship between Tibetans and Chinese in future through better understanding. Time has come to apply our common wisdom in a spirit of tolerance and broad-mindedness to achieve genuine happiness for the Tibetan people with a sense of urgency. On my part, I remain committed to contribute to the welfare of all human beings and in particular the poor and the weak to the best of my ability without making any distinction based on national boundaries.

—Letter to Deng Xiaoping, March 23, 1981

Because of the influence the U.S. can have on developments in China, the solution to the Tibetan problem is also dependent on your actions. U.S. policy toward China must be proactive, not reactive. It must be designed to promote democracy, rule of law, and respect for peoples currently under Chinese Communist rule.

—Address, 1995

Last year a close friend spent some time in Lhasa. After he returned, I inquired where he stayed, and he said with some relatives in the Tibetan quarter. And then I asked him what kind of food he ate for breakfast, and I was a little bit surprised, for he replied to me that in the morning they ate rice. Tibetans, always for breakfast have *tsampa* [roasted barley porridge]. I think every Tibetan, from the Dalai Lama to a beggar, everyone at breakfast chose to have tsampa traditionally. Now, as this story shows, with ordinary Tibetan families in the Lhasa area, their habits are now Chinese. Their whole way of life is now changing, and their mentality also is changing. So, you see the successes of the Chinese leaders and their strategy.

—Address, 1996

Irrespective of whether the Tibetan society before the Chinese occupation was developed in the modern sense or not, the fact remains that, in general, the people did enjoy the basic rights and freedom. On the other hand, the unspeakable suffering that the Tibetans have to endure under Chinese rule is unprecedented in our history. This is a fact which is also commonly recognized by the international community. I have no doubt that the light of truth, freedom, and democracy which is shining unhindered and with growing intensity in different continents will gradually illuminate Tibet as well.

—Message on World Human Rights Day, 1993

The Tibetan struggle is also a nonviolent struggle. We take our inspiration from the teachings of love and compassion of the Buddha, and from the practice of nonviolence of the great leaders, Mahatma Gandhi and Martin Luther King. For me, the path of nonviolence is a matter of principle, and my stand on this is absolutely firm.

—Address, 1995

Today, the freedom struggle of the Tibetan people is at a crucial stage. In recent times the Chinese government has hardened its policies, increased repression in Tibet, and resorted to bullying tactics in addressing the problems of Tibet. Observance of human rights in Tibet has, sadly, not improved. On the contrary, repression and political persecution have lately reached a new peak in Tibet. This has been documented in reports by various international human rights organizations.

—Address, 1996

The future China, while in transition from a totalitarian state to a more open, democratic society, will inevitably have to face the Tibet problem. If the problem is solved properly, it would not only help China's own transition, it could also help bring Tibetans into alliance with China's democratization process. If the issue is not properly solved, China's own transition could be in jeopardy. Resorting to force to suppress a peaceful movement in Tibet would play into the hands of anti-democratic elements in the Chinese society and strengthen their position, damaging China's own efforts to promote a smooth transition.

—Address, 1995

The Chinese came to Tibet not as aggressors but as "liberators." As liberators they should have brought benefits for the Tibetan people. Instead they brought new suffering and destruction. Most of the monasteries have been totally destroyed. If for thirty years the Chinese had adopted a truly friendly attitude, then today the majority of Tibetans would say, "Okay, I'm happy." But that is not the case.

—Address, 1984

For centuries the Tibetan and the Chinese peoples have lived side by side. In future, too, we will have no alternative but to live as neighbors. I have, therefore, always attached great importance to our relationship. In this spirit I have sought to reach out to our Chinese brothers and sisters in the West as well as in Asia.

—Address, 1996

The Tibetan people have a deep trust, believing that the Dalai Lama will bring freedom to them. But I am only a Buddhist monk. I have only the strength of compassion, and the strength that my cause is a just cause.

—Address, 1996

The Chinese have suppressed religious activities so much that the result has been counterproductive. Even older Tibetans are surprised at the degree of religious faith. There is not a single outstanding Communist among today's Tibetan youth. Of the older Tibetans who joined the Communist Party in the 1930s and '40s, nearly all have been disgraced. The young Tibetan Communists are uneducated, simple-minded sycophants. Some can't even read Tibetan. Naturally the people don't respect them and call them "helicopters" because they are promoted so quickly.

—Address, 1984

❧

The sweeping global changes in recent years reaffirm my beliefs for the Tibetan people is now within our reach.

Statement, March 10, 1983

❧

World memory is very short. Within a few years the outside world may forget Tibet, and what has happened there, completely. And then the Chinese leaders would have achieved complete success. Now this we must not allow.

—Address, 1996

❧

If Tibet becomes a zone of peace, it would be a great contribution to the cause of peace in Asia, because India and China are the world's two most populous nations, and it would be a great contribution to peace in the world. Then Tibetan culture and Buddhist culture, that way of life (and not just the Buddhist religion, because there are Tibetan Muslims, too; I am speaking more of a culture, a way of life) is today facing extinction. This culture also has great potential to make a tremendous contribution to peace of mind not only to the six million Tibetan people, but to people all over the world.

—Address, 1995

The Tibetan issue is very much involved with peace in two ways. One, geographically, Tibet is situated between India and China and once Tibet becomes a zone of peace . . . it can make great contributions regarding peace in that part of the world. . . . Then second, the Tibetan culture, usually I describe as a Buddhist culture. It is useful to make a distinction between Buddhism and Buddhist culture. I notice with some Tibetan Muslims, that their way of life, way of thinking, is very much in the way of Buddhist culture. So that culture is basically, I think, of a peaceful nature. The Buddhist culture has the right kind of attitude so that it brings peace with fellow human beings, peace with animals, and peace with the environment. That kind of Buddhist culture I do feel is of great potential, not only benefiting six million Tibetans but also the larger community in that part of the world.

—Address, 1995

Our struggle is not an ideological one. For example, Tibetans do not oppose reforms, communism, and changes.

We don't even harbor ill feeling against the Chinese people as such. We are only struggling for our rights against the illegal occupation of our country by an alien force. We are fighting for justice, the right to govern ourselves, and the freedom to determine our own future. So long as the six million Tibetans are not contented, we will continue our struggle.

—**Message on World Human Rights Day, 1993**

Violations of human rights in Tibet have a distinct character. Such abuses are aimed at Tibetans as a people from asserting their own identity and their wish to preserve it. Thus, human rights violations in Tibet are often the result of institutionalized racial and cultural discrimination. If the human rights situation in Tibet is to be improved, the issue of Tibet should be addressed on its own merits.

—**Address, 1996**

In Tibet our people are being marginalized and discriminated against in the face of creeping sinicization. The undermining and destruction of cultural and religious institutions and traditions coupled with the mass influx of Chinese into Tibet amounts to cultural genocide. The very survival of the Tibetans as a distinct people is under constant threat. Similarly, the issues of environmental destruction, which has serious ramifications beyond the

Tibetan plateau, and indiscriminate economic development must be addressed specifically with regard to Tibet.

—Address, 1996

Sometimes I feel that when we go back to Tibet and things become normal, I will follow Mahatma Gandhi's example. He was a freedom fighter, but once India attained its independence, he did not lead the country.

—Address, 1984

The Dalai Lama is an individual, and even the institution of the Dalai Lama came into being at a certain stage of Tibet's history. In the future it may disappear, but the Tibetan nation will always remain.

—Address, 1985

We Tibetans complain over the fact that China invaded our country and now colonize it. But this isn't because we hate the Chinese. They provided us with a supreme test of courage. Now it is time for them to leave.

—Address, 1986

In spite of the fact that we Tibetans have to oppose Communist China, I can never bring myself to hate her people.

Hatred is not a sign of strength but of weakness. When Lord Buddha said that hatred cannot be overcome by hatred, he was not only being spiritual. But His words reflect the practical reality of life. Whatever one achieves through hatred will not last long. On the other hand, hatred will only generate more problems. And for the Tibetan people who are faced with such a tragic situation, hatred will only bring additional depression. Moreover, how can we hate a people who do not know what they are doing? How can we hate millions of Chinese, who have no power and are helplessly led by their leaders? We cannot even hate the Chinese leaders, for they have suffered tremendously for their nation and the cause which they believe to be right. I do not believe in hatred, but I do believe, as I have always done, that one day truth and justice will triumph.

—Statement, March 10, 1973

We have a right to follow our own destiny, according to our own culture and identity. Nobody has the right to colonize others. I feel that the Buddhist emphasis on love, compassion, and patience has aided us considerably in coming through this difficult period of our history. It has helped us to maintain a sense of clarity, strength, and humor. The Tibetan people can still smile and laugh. They can still look to the future with hope.

—Address, 1996

꙳

I wish to pay homage to the brave men and women of Tibet who have died for the cause of our freedom. I pray also for our compatriots who are enduring mental and physical suffering in Chinese prisons at this moment. Not one day passes without my fervent prayers for an early end to the suffering of our people. I believe that today the question is not whether Tibet will ever be free, but rather how soon.

—Statement, March 10, 1995

꙳

Peace and War

Peace, in the sense of the absence of war, is of little value to someone who is dying of hunger or cold. It will not remove the pain of torture inflicted on a prisoner of conscience. It does not comfort those who have lost their loved ones in floods caused by senseless deforestation in a neighboring country. Peace can last only where human rights are respected, where the people are fed, and where individuals and nations are free. True peace with oneself and with the world around us can be achieved only through the development of mental peace. The other phenomena mentioned above are similarly interrelated.

—Nobel Lecture, 1989

꙳

We have recently seen how newfound freedoms, widely celebrated though they are, have given rise to fresh economic difficulties and unleashed long-buried ethnic and religious tensions that contain the seeds for a new cycle of conflicts. In the context of our newly emerging global community, all forms of violence, especially war, have become totally unacceptable as means of settling disputes. Therefore, it is appropriate to think and to discuss ways of averting further havoc and maintaining the momentum of peaceful and positive change.

—Disarmament, Peace, and Compassion

I heard through BBC that about eighteen million people in Africa face the danger of starvation. Of course, one immediate cause is drought, but another cause is civil war in recent years. A lot of money is being spent on weapons, and agriculture is neglected. All these unfortunate experiences are ultimately related with weapons. The military establishment or wars are part of human history. But I think today things are completely changed, and now we must find some new way of thinking. After all, we have such beautiful human intelligence, but this intelligence certainly is not meant for destruction. If we use our intelligence for destruction, it is really unfortunate.

—"Universal Responsibility and the
Inner Environment"

Our planet is blessed with vast natural treasures. If we use them wisely, beginning with the elimination of militarism and war, every human being will be able to live a healthy, prosperous existence. Naturally, global peace cannot occur all at once. All of us, every member of the world community, has a moral responsibility to help avert the immense suffering which results from war and civil strife. We must find a peaceful, nonviolent way for the forces of freedom, truth, and democracy to develop successfully as peoples emerge from oppression.

—*Disarmament, Peace, and Compassion*

In olden times when there was a war, it was a human-to-human confrontation. The victor in battle would directly see the blood and suffering of the defeated enemy. Nowadays, it is much more terrifying because a man in an office can push a button and kill millions of people and never see the human tragedy he has created. The mechanization of war, the mechanization of human conflict, poses an increasing threat to peace.

—**Address, 1982**

Responsibility does not lie only with the leaders of our countries or with those who have been appointed or elected to do a particular job. It lies with each of us individually. Peace, for example, starts within each one of us. When we have inner peace, we can be at peace with those around us. When our community is in a state of peace, it can share that peace with neighboring communities, and so on. When we feel love and kindness toward others, it not only makes others feel loved and cared for, but it helps us also to develop inner happiness and peace.

—**Nobel Lecture, 1989**

Although war has always been part of human history, in ancient times there were winners and losers. If a nuclear exchange was to occur now, there would be no winners at all. Realizing this danger, steps are being taken to eliminate nuclear weapons. This is a welcome sign. Nonetheless, in a volatile world the risk remains as long as even a handful of these weapons continue to exist.

—*Disarmament, Peace, and Compassion*

Wars arise from a failure to understand one another's humanness. Instead of summit meetings, why not have families meet for a picnic and get to know each other while the children play together?

—**Address, 1984**

The greatest single danger facing all living beings on this planet is the threat of nuclear destruction. Besides this, other problems, whose effects are more gradual, are secondary. At a time of concern for increasing democratic freedoms and human rights, it is contradictory to continue to pursue policies that take little account of every living being's right to life. In the event of nuclear war no one will win, because no one will survive. The key to changing such policies is to increase awareness of the issue.

—*Disarmament, Peace, and Compassion*

There is a growing awareness in the international community of the danger posed by the heavy reliance on military strength and the trade in arms and weapons, including those of mass destruction. Total disarmament will be difficult, but, I believe, necessary in the long run. Costa Rica, a small country in a strategic and very turbulent area, abolished its army in 1948. I am sure most people thought the situation could not last. Yet that country has maintained its integrity without an army for over forty years. Following Costa Rica's lead, your renewed commitment to nonviolence could provide the needed impetus for global disarmament. A principled stand to defend your recently regained freedom without resorting to force would be truly inspiring.

—*Address, 1991*

During the Gulf War crisis the main force came from America. Because of the world situation, the system of collective forces has already happened. In future a policy or military force should be created by nations big or small, irrespectively, but equally balanced forces. These collective forces should be controlled by collective leadership on an international basis. Forces can be mobilized everywhere. If we achieve this, then there will be no more violent conflict between nations, no more civil war. On the other hand, we save a lot of money and also we save a lot of destruction. So fear in the world atmosphere can be reduced to some extent.

—"**Universal Responsibility and the Inner Environment**"

🐭✻

Elimination of violence is not as difficult a task as it may initially appear. Only a small proportion of the world's five billion people are engaged in acts of violence. The overwhelming majority are engaged in acts of loving, caring, and sharing. It is thus my belief that in the human mind the dominant force is not violence, but on the contrary, compassion and peacefulness.

—**Address, 1991**

🐭✻

The anniversary of the bombing of Hiroshima and Naga-saki reminds us of the horrifying nature of nuclear destruction. It is instant, total, and irreversible. Like our neglect and abuse of the natural environment, it has the potential to affect the lives, not only of many defenseless people living now in various parts of the world, but also those of future generations.

—*Disarmament, Peace, and Compassion*

🐭✻

We must control the anger and hatred in ourselves. And as we learn to remain in peace, then we can demonstrate in society in a way that makes a real statement for world peace. If we ourselves remain always angry and then sing world peace, it has little meaning. So, you see, first our individual self must learn peace. This we can practice. Then we can teach the rest of the world.

—*Address, 1984*

Warfare and hatred are always based on misunderstanding about human happiness and on mistrust between people. If the leaders could meet directly, they could start to see each other as people, as human beings, and there would be a chance for some understanding and compassion to grow. Even if these talks were not so friendly at first, they would give an opportunity for this understanding to develop.

—*Address, 1984*

Our ultimate goal should be the demilitarization of the entire planet. If it was properly planned and people were educated to understand its advantages, I believe it would be quite possible. Although we may talk of achieving a global demilitarization, to begin with some kind of inner disarmament is necessary. The key to genuine world peace is inner peace, and the foundation of that is a sense of understanding and respect for each other as human beings, based on compassion and love.

—*Disarmament, Peace, and Compassion*

Once I expressed that I consider the worst event on this planet—in this century—to be the October Revolution in Russia. Because in order to achieve that revolution and in order to sustain that revolution, so much bloodshed happened. Although as far as original Marxism is concerned, I've deep sympathy, in practice and its eventual development, the outcome was so terrible. During certain periods, weapons in general, and particularly nuclear weapons, did some good that we call deterrent. Now the Berlin Wall has collapsed and the Soviet Communist empire has collapsed. That leaves only Communist China. Now there is no danger from Communism, so I think nuclear weapons did their job. Now the time has come to say farewell to these dreadful weapons. We don't need them anymore.

—"**Universal Responsibility and the
Inner Environment**"

On the human level, nobody actually wants war, because it brings unspeakable suffering. Everyone wants peace. But we need a genuine peace. A more genuine peace is founded on mutual trust and the realization that as brothers and sisters we must all live together without trying to destroy each other. Even if one nation or community dislikes another, they have no alternative but to live together. And under the circumstances it is much better to live together happily.

—*Disarmament, Peace, and Compassion*

Whether someone believes something or not, believer or nonbeliever, as long as you are a member of the human family you need warm human feeling, warmhearted feeling. The question of world peace, the question of family peace, the question of peace between wife and husband, or peace between parents and children, everything is dependent on that feeling of love and warmheartedness.

—Address, 1984

You see, technology, science, and economic development must bring some happiness, some good for humanity. I think the time now has gone to thinking only of profit. So within that context we have to think seriously about the war machine, the industry which produces weapons. Particularly nuclear weapons. We have to think very carefully, think seriously. The answer is, I think, that we should pray and we should have some kind of clear vision about the long future, a world without armament, genuine disarmament. Of course, this cannot materialize overnight. Of course, it must come step by step, realistically. But it's very essential to have this idea and vision, and to make an effort on an individual basis, on an organizational basis and, eventually, I think, on a governmental basis.

—"The Need to Balance Spiritual and Material Values"

I think we should seriously think about the arms trade. If we really want genuine peace, we have to think, you see, we have to be prepared. Genuine peace, genuine lasting world peace, can be achieved only through inner peace. Not through more weapons. Of course, in the past nuclear weapons were called deterrents, and, to some extent it worked. But that also I think they kept peace out of fear—that's not genuine peace. Genuine peace must come out of a sense of concern, out of love and compassion and respect. So while we are thinking seriously about the idea of demilitarization, we must at the same time think seriously about inner disarmament. That's through education, through family life, in home as well as in the class, more emphasis on deeper human values, moral principles, self-discipline. And for that, when I say moral principle, I do not necessarily mean involvement in faith, religious faith, but simply involvement in the basis of the reality about human nature and reality of the world.

—''The Need to Balance Spiritual and
Material Values''

War and large military establishments are the greatest sources of violence in our world. Whether their purpose is defensive or offensive, these vast, powerful organizations exist solely to kill human beings. War is neither glamorous nor attractive. Like a fire in the human community, it consumes living beings, and its very nature is one of tragedy and suffering.

—Disarmament, Peace, and Compassion.

When we get seriously ill we need medicine and even sometimes poison is needed. But as soon as one is cured, then these poisonous medicines must be thrown out of the home. To keep them is really dangerous. Now a quite favorable time has come and we should think seriously. First of all we should eliminate nuclear and biological weapons. Eventually we must think seriously about the very concept of war and military establishments. A recent Chinese proposal to totally ban nuclear weapons is good; whether they really stick to it or not is another question. They also carried out a nuclear test recently. That is awful.

—"Universal Responsibility and the
Inner Environment"

As long as we human beings have been here, conflict, disagreement, different views, have also been there. That we can take for granted. So if you follow or if you use violent methods to reduce disagreement or conflict, then we will have, I think, violence every day. Through using violence even more resentment, more dissatisfaction, are sure to come.

—"Compassion, the Basis for
Human Happiness"

Everyone says peace, but when things are related to self-interest, nobody bothers about war, killing, stealing. . . . Under such circumstances you have to be temperate and practical. We need some long-range policy. I feel deeply that maybe we can find some new type of educational system for the younger generation, with an emphasis on love, peace, brotherhood, etc. One or two countries cannot do this; it must be a worldwide movement.

—Address, 1982

Throughout history mankind has pursued peace one way or another. Witnessing the mass slaughter that has occurred in our century has given us the stimulus and opportunity to control war. To do so, it is clear we must disarm. And that can occur only within the context of new political and economic relationships.

—*Disarmament, Peace, and Compassion*

I have always believed that human determination and truth will ultimately prevail over violence and oppression. Today important changes are taking place everywhere in the world which could profoundly affect our future and the future of all humanity and the planet we share. Courageous moves by the world leaders have facilitated the peaceful resolution of conflicts. Hope for peace, for the environment, and for a more human approach to world problems seem greater than ever before.

—Address, 1982

It is worthwhile and important to make an individual effort to stop, or at least to minimize, the danger of war. To begin, of course, we must control the anger and the hatred in ourselves. And as we learn to remain in peace, then we can demonstrate in society in a way that makes a real statement for world peace. If we ourselves remain always angry and then sing world peace, it has little meaning. . . . On a larger scale, those people who really know the danger . . . such as doctors and scientists who can explain clearly, should use their voices and speak up. They might approach it technically, or explain in their own way, so that others will understand. . . . Then, from the spiritual side, they should speak about the importance of preserving human life.

—Address, 1973

These terrible weapons [nuclear arms] cannot function on their own; they require a man's finger to press the fateful button to become operational. The finger itself, as such, is in no position to make a judgment. It is controlled by the brain. The brain is controlled by awareness. So automatically it goes through the heart. If in this place there is hatred, resentment, and wrath, the person can go mad.

In this way the control exercised by love and compassion disappears, and the finger is driven to make a gesture.

—Address, 1985

The awesome proportion of scarce resources squandered on military development not only prevents the elimination of poverty, illiteracy, and disease, but also requires the sacrifice of our scientists' precious human intelligence. Why should their brilliance be wasted in this way when it could be used for positive global development?

—*Disarmament, Peace, and Compassion*

We should think very seriously about the arms trade. War is one way that the producers of weapons get some profit, but if you think closely, there is the other side: the immense suffering. Usually when there is a bombing or some kind of civil war, the first casualties are innocent men and women and children. If these first casualties were the troublemakers, then maybe there might be some justification, but that usually doesn't happen. The real troublemakers remain very comfortable somewhere, and then innocent people suffer.

—''The Need to Balance Spiritual and Material Values''

We talk about peace a great deal. But peace has a chance to exist only when the atmosphere is congenial. We must create that atmosphere. In order to do that we must adopt the right attitude. Peace therefore must basically first come from within ourselves.

—*Address, 1984*

To achieve global demilitarization our first step should be the total dismantling of all nuclear, biological, and chemical weapons. The second step should be the elimination of all offensive arms. And the third step should be the abolition of all national defensive forces. To protect and safeguard humanity from future aggression we can create an international force to which all member states would contribute.

—*Disarmament, Peace, and Compassion*

Before teaching others, before changing others, we ourselves must change. We must be honest, sincere, kindhearted.

—*Address, 1982*

There is a wonderful verse in the Bible about turning swords into plowshares. It's a lovely image, a weapon transformed into a tool to serve basic human needs, symbolic of an attitude of inner and outer disarmament. In the spirit of this ancient message, I think it is important that we stress today the urgency of a policy that is long overdue: the demilitarization of the entire planet.

—**"Universal Responsibility and
Our Global Environment"**

🌿

The problems human society is facing in terms of economic development, the crisis of energy, the tension between the poor and rich nations, and many geopolitical problems can be solved if we understand each other's fundamental humanity, respect each other's rights, share each other's problems and sufferings, and then make a joint effort.

—**Address, 1984**

🌿

Military establishments are destructive not only in times of war. By their very design, they are the single greatest violators of human rights. Once an army has become a powerful force, there is every risk that it will destroy the happiness of its own country. As long as there are powerful armies there will always be the danger of dictatorship.

—*Disarmament, Peace, and Compassion*

🌿

Internal peace is an essential first step to achieving peace in the world, true and lasting peace. How do you cultivate it? It's very simple. In the first place, by realizing clearly that all mankind is one, that human beings in every country are members of one and the same family. In other words, all these quarrels between countries and blocs are family quarrels and should not go beyond certain limits.

—**Address, 1985**

Nations today spend trillions of dollars annually on their military budgets. How many hospital beds, schools, and homes could this money fund?

—*Disarmament, Peace, and Compassion*

Nonviolence

Ahimsa or nonviolence is a powerful idea that Mahatma Gandhi made familiar throughout the world. Nonviolence. It is something more positive, more meaningful than that. The true expression of nonviolence is compassion. Some people seem to think that compassion is just a passive emotional response instead of rational stimulus to action. To experience genuine compassion is to develop a feeling of closeness to others combined with a sense of responsibility for their welfare.

—"**The True Expression of Nonviolence Is Compassion**"

Nonviolence is not just merely the absence of violence. Nonviolence is the opportunity to do harm but to refrain from harming. That is nonviolence. So . . . I consider nonviolence the reflection or manifestation of human love and human compassion. . . . That is nonviolence . . . it is inseparable from like kindness and compassion.

—Address, 1995

From a purely practical perspective, it sometimes seems that by using violence a problem can be solved quite quickly. But if you succeed through violence at the expenses of others' rights and welfare, you have not solved the problem, but only created the seeds for another.

—Address, 1991

Through persistent nonviolent popular efforts dramatic changes, bringing many countries closer to real democracy, have occurred in many places, from Manila in the Philippines to Berlin in East Germany. With the Cold War era apparently drawing to a close, people everywhere live with renewed hope.

—Nobel Lecture, 1989

The human essence of good sense finds no room with anger. Anger, jealousy, impatience, and hatred are the real troublemakers; with them problems cannot be solved. Though one may have temporary success, ultimately one's hatred or anger will create further difficulties. With anger, all actions are swift. When we face problems with compassion, sincerely, and with good motivation, it may take longer, but ultimately the solution is better, for there is far less chance of creating a new problem through the temporary "solution" of the present one.

—*Compassion in Global Politics*

I am a firm believer in nonviolence, on moral as well as practical grounds. Using violence against a strong power can be suicidal. For countries like ours, the only hope for survival is to wage a nonviolent struggle founded on justice, truth, and unwavering determination.

—**Address, 1991**

How does one check anger, hatred? Hatred, ill feeling toward others, and also I think the sense of revenge—those I think are totally negative; almost, I think, absolutely negative. Anger I think can be of two types: hatred with ill feeling is one while another anger—with compassion as the basis of concern—may be positive.

—**"Compassion, the Basis for Human Happiness"**

. . . some of my friends told me that basic human nature is something violent. Then I told my friends, I don't think so. If we examine different mammals, say, those animals such as tigers or lions, who very much depend on others' lives for their basic survival, these animals because of their basic nature have a special structure, their long teeth and long nails, like that. So those peaceful animals, such as deer, which are completely herbivorous, their teeth and nails are something different—more gentle. So from that viewpoint, we human beings belong to the gentle category, isn't that so? Our teeth, or nails, these are very gentle. So I told my friends, I don't agree with your viewpoint. Basically human beings have a nonviolent nature.

—**Address, 1996**

I think it is very important to know two levels of spirituality. One spirituality is faith, religious faith. Another spirituality is without religious faith, but is simply trying to be a warm-hearted person. Try to be a warm-hearted person. So then also with the idea of nonviolence. Once we have cultivated the compassionate mental attitude developed here, then nonviolence automatically comes. Nonviolence is not made up of diplomatic words. Nonviolence is action or acts of compassion. When compassion is here, nonviolent action comes. When hatred is here, violence very often comes.

—**"Compassion, the Basis for Human Happiness"**

As long as I lead our freedom struggle, there will be no deviation from the path of nonviolence.

—**Address, 1995**

True nonviolence . . . means sharing others' view, others' feelings, others' values, and through that way solving problems. So sometimes I tell people, this century, the twentieth century, we call the "Century of Bloodshed," the "Century of War." The result of this is more conflict, more bloodshed, more weapons. So therefore, from the experience which humanity learned from this century, I think the next century should be the "Century of Dialogue." Nonviolent principles will be made available everywhere. And that cannot come through prayer—just sitting here and praying. That's impossible! Work, effort, effort, effort!

—"Compassion, the Basis for
Human Happiness"

In the history of man, it has already been proved that the human will is more powerful than the gun.

—Address, 1985

It is very important to know that anger is negative. Usually people consider anger part of our mind, that it is better to show it, better to let it come. I think that's the wrong conception. Some grievances, due to your past experience, happen only once, or only rarely happen. Then resentment because of grievances may be let out, because then it it finished—that is very possible. Constant anger—that, I think, it is better to check.

—"Compassion, the Basis for
Human Happiness"

🐾

On our part, we Tibetans will continue our nonviolent struggle for freedom. My people are calling for an intensification of the struggle, and I believe they will put this into effect. But we will resist the use of violence as an expression of the desperation which many Tibetans feel.

—Address, 1995

🐾

Anger may seem to offer an energetic way of getting things done, but such a perception of the world is misguided. The only certainty about anger and hatred is that they are destructive; no good ever comes of them. The Chinese students have given me great hope for the future of China and Tibet. I feel that their movement follows the tradition of Mahatma Gandhi's *Ahimsa* or nonviolence, which has deeply inspired me since I was a small boy.

—Address, 1989

🐾

The necessary foundation for world peace and the ultimate goal of any new international order is the elimination of violence at every level. For this reason the practice of nonviolence surely suits us all. It simply requires determination, for by its very nature nonviolent action requires patience. While the practice of nonviolence is still something of an experiment on this planet, if it is successful, it will open the way to a far more peaceful world in the next century.

—Disarmament, Peace, and Compassion

I really have hoped and prayed that the younger generation in this world would take up the cause of truth and nonviolence. I believe that young people have a natural enthusiasm for truth, honesty, and peace. It is basic human nature for young people, who have minds that are very fresh, to have such an inclination.

—Address, 1996

Nonviolence means dialogue, using our language, the human language. Dialogue means compromise: listening to others' views, respecting others' rights; in the spirit of reconciliation there is a real solution to conflict or disagreement. There is no one hundred percent winner, one hundred percent loser—not that way, but half-half. So that is the practical way, that is the only way. Today, I think, the whole world is becoming smaller and smaller. The concept of "we and they" is gone, out of date.

—"Compassion, the Basis for
Human Happiness"

Nonviolence means to be of service to our fellow beings. It is the nature of human beings to yearn for freedom, equality, and dignity. If we accept that others have a right to peace and happiness equal to our own, do we not have a responsibility to help those in need?

—Address, 1995

In order to achieve more effective results and in order to succeed in the protection, conservation, and preservation of the natural environment, first of all, I think, it is also important to bring about internal balance within human beings themselves.

—Address, 1996

It is the enemy who can truly teach us to practice the virtues of compassion and tolerance.

—Address, 1983

One's own anger, pride, and so forth serve as obstacles to the development of one's own altruistic attitude. They harm it. They injure it. Therefore, one shouldn't just let these go on when they are generated, but by relying on antidotes, stop them.

—Address, 1994

In our human life, tolerance is very important. If you have tolerance, you can easily overcome difficulties. If you have little tolerance or are without it, then the smallest thing immediately irritates you. In a difficulty you may overreact. In my own experience I've had many questions, many feelings, and one of these feelings is that tolerance is something to practice worldwide in our human society.

—Address, 1981

The awarding of the Nobel Prize to me, a simple monk from far away Tibet, here in Norway, also fills us Tibetans with hope. It means that despite the fact that we have not drawn attention to our plight by means of violence, we have not been forgotten. It also means that the values we cherish, in particular our respect for all forms of life and the belief in the power of truth, are today recognized and encouraged. It is also a tribute to my mentor, Mahatma Gandhi, whose example is an inspiration to so many of us.

—Nobel Lecture, 1989

Under any circumstances, the Tibetan movement must remain firmly committed to nonviolent, peaceful means. We seek a sustainable relationship with China based on mutual respect and mutual benefit. We seek a long-lasting, good relationship with China. We seek no hostility toward China. If we choose to stay in one country, we should live together as true brothers and sisters. If we choose to be separate, we should become good neighbors. A long-lasting, good relationship with China should always be the top priority of Tibet.

—Address, 1995

I do not agree with people who assert that human beings are innately aggressive, despite the apparent prevalence of anger and hatred in the world.

—"The True Expression of
Nonviolence Is Compassion"

It is said that someone who acts as an enemy toward you is your best teacher. Now, by depending on teachers, you can learn about the importance of being patient, but you can't get any opportunity actually to be patient. However, the actual practice of implementing patience comes when meeting with an enemy.

—Address, 1981

Universal Responsibility

Universal responsibility is the key to human survival. It is the best foundation for world peace.

—"Human Rights and Universal Responsibility"

Man and society are interdependent; hence the quality of man's behavior as an individual and as a participant of his society is inseparable. Reparations have been attempted in the past as contributions to lessening the malaise and dysfunctional attitudes of our social world in order to build a world which is more just and equal. Institutions and organizations have been established with their charter of noble ideology to combat these social problems. For all intents and purposes the objectives have been laudable, but it has been unfortunate that basically good ideas have been defeated by man's inherent self-interest.

—*Place of Ethics and Morality in Politics*

I truly believe that individuals can make a difference in society. Since periods of great change such as the present one come so rarely in human history, it is up to each of us to make the best use of our time to help create a happier world.

—Address, 1992

Nevertheless, no one can afford to assume that someone else will solve our problems. Every individual has a responsibility to help guide our human family in the right direction. Good wishes are not sufficient; we must assume responsibility. Since periods of great change such as the present one come so rarely in human history, it is up to each of us to use our time well to help create a happier, more peaceful world.

—*Disarmament, Peace, and Compassion*

Irrespective of varying degrees of development and economic disparities, continents, nations, communities, families, in fact, all individuals are dependent on one another for their existence and well-being. Every human being wishes for happiness and does not want suffering. By clearly realizing this, we must develop mutual compassion, love, and a fundamental sense of justice. In such an atmosphere there is hope that problems between nations and problems within families can be gradually overcome and that people can live in peace and harmony. Instead, if people adopt an attitude of selfishness, domination, and jealousy, the world at large, as well as individuals, will never enjoy peace and harmony. Therefore, I believe that human relations based on mutual compassion and love is fundamentally important to human happiness.

—Address, 1984

Basically, every human individual carries responsibility for the benefit or welfare of humanity and for the planet itself, because this planet is our only home. We have no alternative refuge. Therefore, everyone has the responsibility to care not only for our fellow human beings but also for insects, plants, animals, and this very planet. However, the initiative must come from individuals. But then, in order to make an impact, the unified mobilization of individual forces through various organizations is the only path.

—"**Universal Responsibility and the Inner Environment**"

In society today, particularly toward younger people, the media has a great, great responsibility. I have always believed that on this planet we are one human family, and now because of many new factors today, the concepts of "they" and "we" should be gone. We have to think of the entire human race as "we." There is no more "my interest" or "your interest"; all of our interests are related to the whole world, to all people, including the media. We are now one global family, so when there is a problem or a threat to one of us, all of us will suffer. There is no escape. We all have the responsibility to look after the world.

—**Address, 1995**

Whether we like it or not, we have all been born on this earth as part of one great family. Rich or poor, educated or uneducated, belonging to one nation, religion, ideology, or another, ultimately each of us is just a human being like everyone else. We all desire happiness and do not want suffering. Furthermore, each of us has the same right to pursue happiness and avoid suffering. When you recognize that all beings are equal in this respect, you automatically feel empathy and closeness for them. Out of this, in turn, comes a genuine sense of universal responsibility; the wish to actively help others overcome their problems.

—"**Universal Responsibility and Our Global Environment**"

Now that the world has become a much smaller place, much depends on each of us. In order to go forward positively, the main factor is human mind, human consciousness. So here, the sense of commitment toward a better future world, that sort of sense of responsibility, that is our real hope. All professions should play a role—educators, religious leaders, economists, and of course politicians. They all have different activities, but they must be for humanity, because now when we talk about humanity we cannot make a distinction between us versus them.

—**Address, 1995**

To counteract these harmful practices we can teach ourselves to be more aware of our own mutual dependence. Every sentient being wants happiness instead of pain. So we all share a common basic feeling. We can develop right actions to help the Earth and each other based on a better motivation. Therefore, I always speak of the importance of developing a genuine sense of universal responsibility.

—"**Thinking Globally: A Universal Task**"

During the course of my extensive traveling to countries across the world, rich and poor, East and West, I have seen people reveling in pleasure and people suffering. The advancement of science and technology seems to have achieved little more than linear, numerical improvement; development often means little more than more mansions in more cities. As a result, the ecological balance—the very basis of our life on earth—has been greatly affected. On the other hand, in days gone by, the people of Tibet lived a happy life, untroubled by pollution, in natural conditions.

—*The Sheltering Tree*

We can no longer invoke the national, racial, or ideological barriers that separate us without destructive repercussions. In the context of our new interdependence, considering the interests of others is clearly the best form of self-interest. Interdependence, of course, is a fundamental law of nature. Not only myriad forms of life, but the most subtle level of material phenomena as well, is governed by interdependence. All phenomena, from the planet we inhabit to the oceans, clouds, forests, and flowers that surround us, arise in dependence upon subtle patterns of energy. Without their proper interaction they dissolve and decay.

—"**Universal Responsibility and Our Global Environment**"

I, for one, strongly believe that individuals can make a difference in society. Every individual has a responsibility to help move our global family in the right direction, and we must each assume that responsibility. As a Buddhist monk I try to develop compassion within myself, not simply as a religious practice, but on a human level as well. To encourage myself in this altruistic attitude, I sometimes find it helpful to imagine myself standing as a single individual on one side, facing a huge gathering of all other human beings on the other side. Then I ask myself, "Whose interests are more important?" To me it is quite clear that however important I may feel I am, I am just one individual while others are infinite in number and importance.

—"**Human Rights and Universal Responsibility**"

To act altruistically, concerned only for the welfare of others, with no selfish or ulterior motives, is to affirm a sense of universal responsibility.

—"**The True Expression of Nonviolence Is Compassion**"

Our world is becoming smaller and ever more interdependent with the rapid growth in population and increasing contact between people and governments. In this light, it is important to reassess the rights and responsibilities of individuals, peoples, and nations in relation to each other and to the planet as a whole.

—"Human Rights and Universal Responsibility"

The global economy too is becoming increasingly integrated so that the results of an election in one country can affect the stock market of another. In ancient times, each village was more or less self-sufficient and independent. There was neither the need nor the expectation of cooperation with others outside the village. You survived by doing everything yourself. The situation now has completely changed. It has become very old-fashioned to think only in terms of my nation or my country, let alone my village. Universal responsibility is the real key to overcoming our problems.

—"The True Expression of
Nonviolence Is Compassion"

I think human harmony is based on a true sense of brotherhood. As a Buddhist, it doesn't matter whether we are believers or nonbelievers, educated or uneducated, Easterners or Westerners or Northerners or Southerners, as long as we are the same human beings with the same kind of features. Everyone wants happiness and doesn't want sorrow, and we have every right to be very happy.

—Address, 1985

If you must be selfish, then be wise and not narrow-minded in your selfishness. The key point lies in the sense of universal responsibility. That is the real source of strength, the real source of happiness. If we exploit everything available, such as trees, water, and minerals, and if we don't plan for our next generation, for the future, then we're at fault, aren't we? However, if we have a genuine sense of universal responsibility as our central motivation, then our relations with the environment, and with all our neighbors, will be well balanced.

—*Humanity and Ecology*

I often joke that the moon and stars look beautiful, but if any of us tried to live on them we would be miserable. This blue planet of ours is a delightful habitat. Its life is our life, its future our future. Indeed, the earth acts like a mother to us all. Like children, we are dependent on her. In the face of such global problems as the greenhouse effect and depletion of the ozone layer, individual organizations and single nations are helpless. Unless we all work together, no solution can be found. Our mother earth is teaching us a lesson in universal responsibility.

—**"Universal Responsibility and
Our Global Environment"**

As I mentioned earlier, many forms of human activity, like religion, politics, technology, science, and law, are supposedly meant for the betterment and happiness of humanity. Because of past experience many people feel that politics is something dirty. That is also a wrong concept. In a democratic country practicing democracy effectively, whether we like it or not, political parties must be there. Under such circumstances, if you remain removed from politics, just to criticize or complain, or resent, that is not a wise way.

—"**Universal Responsibility and the Inner Environment**"

I feel that the essence of all spiritual life is your emotion, your attitude toward others. Once you have pure and sincere motivation, all the rest follows. You can develop this right attitude toward others on the basis of kindness, love, and respect, and on the clear realization of the oneness of all human beings. This is important because others benefit by this motivation as much as anything we do. Then, with a pure heart, you can carry on any work— farming, mechanical engineering, working as a doctor, as a lawyer, as a teacher—and your profession becomes a real instrument to help the human community.

—**Address, 1983**

What we need now is a holistic approach toward problems with a genuine sense of universal responsibility based on love and compassion.

—"**Caring for the Earth**"

✤

Everyone has the right to be a happy person and the right to overcome suffering. After all, the purpose of our very life, I consider, is happiness. This is our birthright. Then, because of the changing situation today, the realization of oneness of all human beings is now very relevant. In ancient times, if you had that kind of perspective, good; if not, it did not matter. But now, today, in reality, whether we like it or not every crisis is essentially linked to a global crisis. So talking about my nation, my continent, my family, my religion, my tradition, is out of date. Therefore, there is really an urgent need to have a sense of universal responsibility and change of our inner environment.

—**"Universal Responsibility and the Inner Environment"**

✤

If you think in a deeper way that you are going to be selfish, then be wisely selfish, not narrow-mindedly selfish. From that viewpoint, the key thing is the sense of universal responsibility, that is, the real source of strength, the real source of happiness. From that perspective, if in our generation we exploit every available thing, trees, water, mineral resources, or anything, without bothering about the next generation, about the future, that's our guilt, isn't it? So if we have a genuine sense of universal responsibility as the central motivation and principle, then from that direction our relations with the environment will be well balanced. Similarly with every aspect of relationships: our relations with our neighbors, our family neighbors or country neighbors, will be balanced from that direction.

—**Address, 1996**

❦

We do not need to become religious, nor do we need to believe in an ideology. All that is necessary is for each of us to develop our good human qualities. The need for a sense of universal responsibility affects every aspect of modern life.

—**"Universal Responsibility and
Our Global Environment"**

❦

Real, true brotherhood, a good heart toward one's fellow men, this is the basic thing. I believe that if you have a true feeling of brotherhood, then whether you are a scientist, an economist, or a politician, whatever profession you may follow, you will always have this concern for your fellow beings. I also believe that if you have this concern for others, then whatever the effects that might result from the profession you follow, you will always be concerned as to whether it is going to benefit or harm your fellow beings.

—**Address, 1973**

❦

I think we say that because of the lessons we have begun to learn, the next century will be friendlier, more harmonious, and less harmful. Compassion, the seeds of peace, will be able to flourish. I am very hopeful. At the same time I believe that every individual has a responsibility to help guide our global family in the right direction. Good wishes alone are not enough; we have to assume responsibility. Large human movements spring from individual human initiatives.

—"**Universal Responsibility and
Our Global Environment**"

Universal responsibility is the feeling for other people's suffering just as we feel our own. It is the realization that even our own enemy is motivated by the quest for happiness. We must recognize that all beings want the same thing we want. This is the way to achieve a true understanding, unfettered by artificial consideration.

—"**The True Expression of
Nonviolence Is Compassion**"

Each of us must learn to work not just for his or her own self, family, or nation, but for the benefit of all mankind. Universal responsibility is the real key to human survival. It is the best foundation for world peace, the equitable use of natural resources and, through concern for future generations, the proper care of the environment.

—"**Universal Responsibility and
Our Global Environment**"

In this century we have seen enough war, poverty, pollution, and suffering. According to Buddhist teaching, such things happen as the result of ignorance and selfish actions, because we often fail to see the essential common relation of all beings. The Earth is showing us warnings and clear indications of the vast effects and negative potential of misdirected human behavior.

—"**Thinking Globally: A Universal Task**"

Come together and think in terms of one world.

—"**Universal Responsibility and the Inner Environment**"

At the global level, trees and forests are closely linked with weather patterns and also the maintenance of a crucial balance in nature. Hence, the task of environmental protection is a universal responsibility of all of us. I think that it is extremely important for the Tibetans living in the settlements to not only take a keen interest in the cause of environmental protection, but also to implement this ideal in action by planting new trees. In this way we will be making an important gesture to the world in demonstrating our global concern and at the same time making our own little, but significant, contribution to the cause.

—"**The Importance of Tree Planting and Its Protection**"

⚜

The development of human society is based entirely on people helping each other. Every individual has a responsibility to help guide the community in the right direction, and we must each assume that responsibility.

—"The True Expression of
Nonviolence Is Compassion"

⚜

Human Rights

A human society without laws aimed at establishing justice will find itself enmeshed in suffering. The strong will impose their will upon the weak, the wealthy upon the poor, the governing upon the governed. So justice is something very important within society. If we lose sight of it, we ourselves will greatly suffer as a result.

—*Justice and Society*

⚜

Recently, the United States has led the international community in freeing a small country from a cruel occupation. I am happy for the people of Kuwait. Sadly, all small nations cannot expect similar support for their rights and freedoms. However, I believe that a "new world order" cannot truly emerge unless it is matched by a "new world freedom." Order without freedom is repression. Freedom without order is anarchy. We need both a new world

order that prohibits aggression and a new world freedom
that supports the liberty of individuals and nations.

—Address, 1991

⁂

No matter what country or continent we come from, we
are all basically the same human beings. We have common human needs and concerns. We all seek happiness
and try to avoid suffering regardless of our race, religion,
sex, or political status. Human beings, indeed all sentient
beings, have the right to pursue happiness and live in
peace and in freedom. As free human beings we can use
our unique intelligence to try to understand ourselves
and our world. But if we are prevented from using our
creative potential, we are deprived of one of the basic
characteristics of a human being. It is very often the most
gifted, dedicated, and creative members of our society
who become victims of human rights abuses. Thus the
political, social, cultural, and economic developments of
a society are obstructed by violations of human rights.
Therefore, the protection of these rights and freedoms are
of immense importance both for the individuals affected
and for the development of the society as a whole.

—"Human Rights and Universal Responsibility"

⁂

Plainly speaking, when I began speaking about the value
of human beings, universal human values, and compassionate society, I did not really expect a response from the
younger generation, and certainly not with such a deep

commitment. I very much appreciate that young people have decided to help me to work for basic human rights for all humanity, and respect for human dignity. Of course, this movement is not easy, and there may be many obstacles, not necessarily due to direct opposition, but due to indifference, people being indifferent to basic human values.

—Address, 1986

I believe in justice and truth, without which there would be no basis for human hope.

—Statement, March 10, 1974

The dramatic changes in the past few years clearly indicate that the triumph of human rights is inevitable. There is a growing awareness of people's responsibilities to each other and to the planet we share. This is encouraging even though so much suffering continues to be inflicted based on chauvinism, race, religion, ideology, and history.

—"Human Rights and Universal Responsibility"

Violations of human rights in Tibet have a distinct character. Such abuses are aimed at Tibetans as a people from asserting their own identity and their wish to preserve it. Thus, human rights violations in Tibet are often the result of institutionalized racial and cultural discrimination.

—**Address, 1996**

🦎

Happiness is man's prerogative. He seeks it and each man is equally entitled to his pursuit of happiness; no man seeks misery. Justice and equality belongs to man's prerogatives too, but ones which should derive their practice from altruism and which have not been corroded by the stations of power and wealth. In order to build such an altruistic motivation so that justice and equality may co-exist in truth, the creation of a staunch moral fabric for the social environment is a prerequisite. Concerned voices are being raised about this inherent vacuum in the moral foundation of today, since this lack is the foremost deterrent to a just and equal world.

—*Place of Morality and Ethics in Politics*

🦎

We are witnessing a tremendous popular movement for the advancement of human rights and democratic freedom in the world. This movement must become an even more powerful moral force so that even the most obstructive governments and armies are incapable of suppressing it.

—**"Human Rights and Universal Responsibility"**

🦎

Within each nation the individual's inalienable right to happiness ought to be recognized, and among different nations there must be equal concern for the welfare of even the smallest nation. I am not suggesting that one system is better than another and that all should adopt it. On the contrary, a variety of political systems and ideologies is desirable to enrich the human community, as long as all people are free to evolve their own political and socioeconomic system, based on self-determination. If people in poor countries are denied the happiness they desire and deserve, they will naturally be dissatisfied and pose problems for the rich. If unwanted social, political, and cultural forms continue to be imposed by one nation upon another, the attainment of world peace is doubtful.

—Address, 1985

Some people think that causing pain to others may lead to their own happiness or that their own happiness is of such importance that the pain of others is of no significance. But this is clearly shortsighted. No one truly benefits from causing harm to another being. Whatever immediate advantage is gained at the expense of someone else is short-lived. In the long run causing others misery and infringing upon their peace and happiness creates anxiety, fear, and suspicion for oneself.

—"Human Rights and Universal Responsibility"

I think human rights in general, and particularly women's rights, are very important. Here I feel, in certain fields, we still have traces of the inhumanity, the old uncivilized thinking.

—Address, 1995

🌿

Throughout human history, dictators and totalitarian governments have learned that there is nothing more powerful than a people's yearning for freedom and dignity. While bodies may be enslaved or imprisoned, the human spirit can never be subjugated or defeated. As long as we uphold this human spirit and determination, our aspirations and beliefs have the power to ultimately prevail.

—Statement, March 10, 1983

🌿

Now, obviously every human being in nature has a feeling of "I." That is right, we cannot explain why that feeling is there, but there is no doubt that feeling is there. There is the desire for happiness, desire to overcome suffering; also we have the right to achieve happiness, the maximum happiness, and also we have the right to overcome suffering with that motivation.

—"Compassion, the Basis for
Human Happiness"

🌿

Brute force, no matter how strongly applied, can never subdue the basic human desire for freedom and dignity.

—"Human Rights and Universal Responsibility"

Women must take every advantage of every opportunity and make themselves equal in every field through education or through training or whatever way. I think it is important.

—Address, 1995

The suppression of the rights and freedoms of any people by totalitarian governments is against human nature, and the recent movement for democracy in various parts of the world is a clear indication of this.

—Address, 1988

By any social, moral, religious, or legal standards the theft of one individual's property by another is universally condemned; so is the suppression of that individual's rights and natural freedom. Surely, when this same act of robbery and oppression is committed by one race against another, it can only be considered a crime of immense magnitude.

—*The True Face of Tibet*

A new hope is emerging for the downtrodden, and people everywhere are displaying a willingness to champion and defend the rights and freedoms of their fellow human beings.

—"**Human Rights and Universal Responsibility**"

Discrimination against persons of a different race, against women, and against weaker sections of society may be traditional in some places, but because they are inconsistent with universally recognized human rights, these forms of behavior should change. The universal principle of the equality of all human beings must take precedence.

—**Address, 1988**

The right to express one's ideas and to make every effort to implement them enables people anywhere to become creative and progressive. This engenders human society to make rapid progress and experience genuine harmony. When differences of opinion are frankly expressed and thoroughly discussed, instead of keeping them within one's breast, there is no need to grab an opportunity to topple one another with deep-rooted hatred.

—**Statement, March 10, 1983**

We need to think in global terms because the effects of one nation's actions are felt far beyond its borders. The acceptance of universally binding standards of human rights as laid down in the Universal Declaration of

Human Rights and in the International Covenants of Human Rights is essential in today's shrinking world. Respect for fundamental human rights should not remain an ideal to be achieved but a requisite foundation for every human society. When we demand the rights and freedoms we so cherish, we should also be aware of our responsibilities. If we accept that others have an equal right to peace and happiness as ourselves, do we not have a responsibility to help those in need? Respect for fundamental human rights is as important to the people of Africa and Asia as it is to those in Europe or the Americas.

—"**Human Rights and Universal Responsibility**"

People somehow have become accustomed to the lack of respect for human rights and for each other that is so prevalent in the world today. But we can see that there is something wrong with the way things are; there is definitely something lacking. So we are trying to reach the minds of such people who cannot envision anything better. Many people when they are listening might think, "Oh, this is some kind of young person's attitude, so unrealistic." Therefore, I think it is important that we persist in our efforts, despite the many obstacles that we will encounter.

—**Address, 1996**

A dynamic revolution is deemed crucial for instigating a political culture founded on moral ethics; such a revolution must be sponsored by the powerful nations, for any such attempt by the smaller and the weaker nations is unlikely to succeed. If powerful nations adopt policies based on a bedrock of moral principles and if they concern themselves genuinely with the welfare of mankind, a new path and a new ray of hope will emerge. Such a revolution will surpass all other attempts to achieve justice and equality in our world.

—Place of Morality and Ethics in Politics

It is not only our right as members of the global human family to protest when our brothers and sisters are being treated brutally, but it is also our duty to do whatever we can to help them.

—**"Human Rights and Universal Responsibility"**

China needs human rights, democracy, and the rule of law. These values are the foundation of a free and dynamic society. They are also the source of true peace and stability.

—**Address, 1996**

All human beings, whatever their cultural or historical background, suffer when they are intimidated, imprisoned, or tortured. The question of human rights is so fundamentally important that there should be no difference of views on this. We must therefore insist on a global consensus not only on the need to respect human rights worldwide but more importantly on the definition of these rights.

—"**Human Rights and Universal Responsibility**"

It is undoubtedly in the interest of the Chinese people that the present totalitarian one-party state give way to a democratic system in which fundamental human rights and freedoms are protected and promoted. The people of China have clearly manifested their desire for human rights, democracy, and the rule of law in successive movements starting in 1979 with the Democracy Wall and culminating in the great popular movement of the spring of 1989.

—**Address, 1996**

It is my belief that in human society the fulfillment of basic needs, such as food, shelter, and clothing, alone is not sufficient. If you observe them, it is clear that animals experience a sense of satisfaction when well fed, sheltered, and kindly treated. But for human beings, the freedom to hold and express personal views is without doubt an essential ingredient for genuine happiness. To a distinct people with a long history, a rich culture, and a deep spiritual tradition like ours, freedom is an inalienable right which can never be replaced or assuaged by temporary improvements in economic conditions.

—*The True Face of Tibet*

❧

The right to express one's ideas and to make every effort to implement them enables people everywhere to become creative and progressive. This engenders human society to make rapid progress and experience genuine harmony. . . . The deprivation of freedom to express one's views, either by force or by other means, is absolutely anachronistic and a brutal form of oppression. . . . The people of the world will not only oppose it, but will condemn it. Hence, the six million Tibetan people must have the right to preserve and enhance their cultural destiny and manage their own affairs, and find fulfillment of their free self-expression, without interference from any quarters. This is reasonable and just.

—Address, 1983

❧

When I was a small boy living in Tibet, President Roosevelt sent me a gift: a gold watch showing phases of the moon and the days of the week. I marveled at the distant land which could make such a practical object so beautiful. But what truly inspired me were your ideals of freedom and democracy. I felt that your principles were identical to my own, the Buddhist beliefs in fundamental human rights—freedom, equality, tolerance, and compassion for all.

—Address, 1991

❧

Diversity and traditions can never justify the violations of human rights. Thus, discrimination of persons from a different race, of women, and of weaker sections of society may be traditional in some regions, but if they are inconsistent with universally recognized human rights, these forms of behavior must change.

—"**Human Rights and Universal Responsibility**"

Our rich diversity of cultures and traditions should help to strengthen fundamental human rights in all communities. Mere tradition can never justify violations of human rights.

—**Address, 1988**

It is not enough, as communist systems have assumed, merely to provide people with food, shelter, and clothing. The deeper human nature needs to breathe the precious air of liberty. However, some governments still consider the fundamental human rights of its citizens an internal matter of the state.

—"**Human Rights and Universal Responsibility**"

A society upholding values (of civil rights, law, and democracy) will offer far greater potential and security for trade and investment. A democratic China is thus also in the interest of the international community in general and of Asia in particular. Therefore, every effort should be made not only to integrate China into the world economy, but also to encourage her to enter the mainstream of global democracy. Nevertheless, freedom and democracy in China can be brought about only by the Chinese themselves, not by anyone else. This is why the brave and dedicated members of the Chinese democracy movement deserve our encouragement and support.

—**Address, 1995**

🪴

The universal principles of equality of all human beings must take precedence. It is mainly the authoritarian and totalitarian regimes that are opposed to the universality of human rights. It would be absolutely wrong to concede to this view. On the contrary, such regimes must be made to respect and conform to the universally accepted principles in the larger and long-term interests of their own peoples.

—**"Human Rights and Universal Responsibility"**

🪴

On my last trip to the United States I was taken to Independence Hall in Philadelphia. I was profoundly inspired to stand in the chamber from which your Declaration of Independence and Constitution came. I was then shown to the main floor before the Liberty Bell. My guide explained that two hundred years ago this bell pealed forth to proclaim liberty throughout your land. On examining it, however, I couldn't help noticing the crack in the bell. That crack, I feel, is a reminder to the American people, who enjoy so much freedom while people in other parts

of the world, such as Tibet, have no freedom. The Liberty
Bell is a reminder that you cannot be truly free until people everywhere are free. I believe that this reminder is
alive, and that your great strength continues to come
from your deep principles.

—**Address, 1991**

🌺

In order to achieve genuine happiness in any human society, freedom of thought is extremely important. This
freedom of thought can be achieved only from mutual
trust, mutual understanding, and the absence of fear. . . .
In the case of Tibet and China too, unless we can remove
the state of mutual fear and mistrust, unless we can develop a genuine sense of friendship and goodwill, the
problems that we face today will continue to exist.

—**Address, 1994**

🌺

Fundamental human rights and democratic freedoms
must be respected in Tibet. The Tibetan people must once
again be free to develop culturally, intellectually, economically, and spiritually, and to exercise basic democratic
freedoms. Human rights violations in Tibet are among
the most serious in the world. Discrimination is practiced
in Tibet under a policy of apartheid which the Chinese
call "segregation and assimilation." Tibetans are, at best,
second-class citizens in their own country. Deprived of all
basic democratic rights and freedoms, they exist under a
colonial administration in which all real power is wielded

by Chinese officials of the Communist Party and the army.

—**Five Point Peace Plan**

Environment

Our ancestors viewed the earth as rich and bountiful, which it is. Many people in the past also saw nature as inexhaustibly sustainable, which we know is the case only if we care for it. It is not difficult to forgive destruction in the past which resulted from ignorance. Today, however, we have access to more information; it is essential that we reexamine ethically what we have inherited, what we are responsible for, and what we will pass on to coming generations. Many of the earth's habitats, animals, plants, insects, and even microorganisms that we know to be rare may not be known at all by future generations. We have the capability and the responsibility to act; we must do so before it is too late.

—*Humanity and Ecology*

Destruction of nature and natural resources results from ignorance, greed, and lack of respect for the earth's living things. . . . This lack of respect extends even to earth's human descendants, the future generations who will inherit a vastly degraded planet if world peace does not become a reality, and destruction of the natural environment continues at the present rate.

—An Ethical Approach to
Environmental Protection

When forests are destroyed, many beings . . . also become refugees. However, even greater is the threat that due to such actions climatic patterns are altered all over this planet. When this occurs the very basis of life on this planet could be affected.

—Statement on Timber Cutting

I think one danger is that things like nuclear war are an immediate cause of concern, so everybody realizes something is horrible. But damage to the environment happens gradually, without much awareness. Once we realize this and it becomes very obvious to everybody, it may be too late. So therefore I think we must realize, in time, our responsibility to take care of our own world. I often tell people that the moon and the stars when remaining high in the sky look very beautiful, like an ornament. But if we really try to go and settle there on the moon, perhaps a few days may be very nice and some new experience may be very exciting. But if we really remain there, I think we would soon get very homesick for our small planet. So this is our only home. Therefore, I think this kind of gathering concerning our environment and the planet is very useful, very important and timely.

—Address, 1992

We need knowledge to care for ourselves, every part of the Earth and the life upon it, and all of the future generations as well. This means that education about the environment is of great importance to everyone.

"Thinking Globally: A Universal Task"

For this generation and for future generations, the environment is very important. If we exploit the environment in extreme ways, we will suffer, as will our future generations.

—*Humanity and Ecology*

Our marvels of science and technology are matched, if not outweighed, by many current tragedies, including human starvation in some parts of the world and extinction of other life forms. Many of Earth's habitats, animals, and plants that we know as rare may not be known at all by future generations. We have the capability and the responsibility. We must act before it is too late.

—Address, 1973

These threatening developments are individually drastic and together amazing. The world's population has tripled in this century alone and is expected to double or triple in the next. The global economy may grow by a factor of five or ten, including with it extreme rates of energy consumption, carbon dioxide production, and deforestation. It is hard to imagine all of these things actually happening in our lifetime and in the lives of our children. We have to consider the prospects of global suffering and environment degradation unlike anything in human history.

"Thinking Globally: A Universal Task"

Since I deeply believe that basically human beings are of a gentle nature, I think the human attitude toward our environment should be gentle. Therefore I believe that not only should we keep our relationships with other fellow human beings very gentle and nonviolent, in the same way it is also very important to extend that kind of attitude toward the natural environment. I think morally speaking we can think like that and we should all be concerned for our environment. Then I think there is another viewpoint. In this case it is not a question of morality or ethics, but is a question of our own survival. Not only this generation, but for future generations, the environment is very important. . . . If we exploit the natural environment in an extreme way, today we might get some benefit, but in the long run we ourselves will suffer and other generations will suffer.

—Address, 1996

If we look around, we can now see that those houses in the monasteries and in various camps where people have planted fruit trees now enjoy great benefits as a consequence of their action. First of all, if there is a tree in your courtyard, it creates around it an atmosphere of natural beauty and serenity. It is also obvious that you can eat the fruits from the tree, sit under it and enjoy the cool shade. What was required on your part was a little patience to allow some time for the tree to grow up.

"The Importance of Tree Planting
and Its Protection"

When the environment changes, the climatic condition also changes. When the climate changes dramatically, the economy and many other things change. Our physical health will be greatly affected. Again, conservation is not merely a question of morality, but a question of our own survival.

—*Humanity and Ecology*

The Earth is not only the common heritage of all humankind but also the ultimate source of life. By overexploiting its resources we are undermining the very basis of our own life. All around, signs of the destruction caused by human activity and of the degradation of nature abound. Therefore, the protection and conservation of the Earth is not a question of morality or ethics but a question of our own survival. How we respond to this challenge will affect not only this generation but many generations to come.

—*Caring for the Earth*

₹✺

Today, all over the world, including Tibet, ecological deg-radation is fast overtaking us. I am wholly convinced that if all of us do not make a concerted effort, with a sense of universal responsibility, we will see the gradual break-down of the fragile ecosystems that support us, resulting in an irreversible and irrevocable degradation of our planet Earth.

—*The Sheltering Tree*

₹✺

It has been said in the writings of Je Tsonkapa that who-soever destroys a tree commits a thousand murders. Even though these individuals believe that this is their only life, their belief does not in any way affect the universal laws of karma, cause and effect, and of rebirth. I assure you as head of the Gelukpa lineage and the religious leader of Tibet and the Tibetan people in exile that karma is a real-ity and that rebirth is a reality and that whosoever is re-sponsible for the cutting of even one redwood tree will spend many lifetimes in the lower realms as a hungry ghost or as a hell being. This is what the Buddha taught.

—*Statement on Timber Cutting*

₹✺

No one knows what will happen in a few decades or a few centuries, what adverse effect, for example, deforestation might have on the weather, the soil, the rain.

—*Address, 1986*

If we exploit everything available, such as trees, water, and minerals, and if we don't plan for our next generation, for the future, then we're at fault, aren't we? However, if we have a genuine sense of universal responsibility as our central motivation, then our relations with the environment, and with all our neighbors, will be well balanced.

—Humanity and Ecology

Because of the growth in population, a large number of trees are cut for fuel, and to reclaim land for agricultural cultivation. In the case of Tibet, too, the Chinese have now destroyed its ancient trees in a similar way as if a man's hair has been shaved off. This is not just the destruction of the trees, but it also means harming what belongs to the Tibetans. Similarly, the continuing decline in forests in many parts of the world, including America, is adversely affecting the already changing global climate, thus upsetting the lives of not only mankind but also of all living beings.

**"A Green Environment for
Now and the Future"**

Peace and the survival of life on earth as we know it are threatened by human activities which lack a commitment to humanitarian values.

*—An Ethical Approach to
Environmental Protection*

❧

We should extend this attitude to be concerned for our whole environment. As a basic principle, I think it is better to help if you can, and if you cannot help, at least try not to do harm. This is an especially suitable guide when there is so much yet to understand about the complex interrelations of diverse and unique ecosystems. The Earth is our home and our mother. We need to respect and take care of her. It is easy to understand why.

"Thinking Globally: A Universal Task"

❧

In order to achieve more effective environmental protection and conservation, internal balance within the human being himself or herself is essential.

—*Humanity and Ecology*

❧

We are having problems because people are concentrating on their selfish interests, on making money, and not thinking of the community as a whole. They are not thinking of the Earth and the long-term effects on man as a whole. If we of the present generation do not think about them now, the future generation might not be able to cope with them.

—*Address, 1985*

❧

I can only say therefore it is the duty of every human being, and particularly those who have belief in the Buddhist Dharma, to protect life and to use any legal means possible to prevent the further cutting of forests, and to make public the grasping rapaciousness of those individuals and companies, syndicates, and consortiums who are responsible.

—Statement on Timber Cutting

Just as we should cultivate gentle and peaceful relations with our fellow human beings, we should also extend that same kind of attitude toward the natural environment. Morally speaking, we should be concerned for our whole environment.

—Address, 1973

Scientific predictions of environmental change are difficult for ordinary human beings to comprehend fully. We hear about hot temperatures and rising sea levels, increasing cancer rates, vast population growth, depletion of resources, and extinction of species. Human activity everywhere is hastening to destroy key elements of the natural ecosystems all living beings depend on.

''Thinking Globally: A Universal Task''

The rapacious cutting of timber, the destruction of the rain forests and other forest areas, can only be defined as a threat against existence on this planet and a crime against the continued existence of the human race. We, as refugees from the Communist Chinese and their totalitarian government, know what it is to be without a home.

—Statement on Timber Cutting

ϟ✿

The negligence of the environment, which has resulted in great harm to the human community, resulted from our ignorance of the very special importance of the environment. We must now help people to understand the need for environmental protection. We must teach people to understand the need for environmental protection. We must teach people that conservation directly aids our survival.

—Humanity and Ecology

ϟ✿

Peace and the survival of life on Earth as we know it are threatened by human activities that lack a commitment to humanitarian values. Destruction of nature and natural resources results from ignorance, greed, and lack of respect for the Earth's living things.

—Address, 1973

ϟ✿

In the past the mountains of Tibet had very thick snow. Older people say that these mountains were covered with thick snow when they were young and that the snows are getting thinner, which may be an indication of the end of the world. It is a fact that climatic change is a slow process taking thousands of years to realize its effect. Living beings and plant life on this planet also undergo change accordingly. Man's physical structure too changes from generation to generation along with the change in climatic conditions.

*"A Green Environment for
Now and the Future"*

Ultimately, the decision to save the environment must come from the human heart. The key point is a call for a genuine sense of universal responsibility that is based on love, compassion, and clear awareness.

—Humanity and Ecology

Ancient cultures that have adapted to their natural surroundings can offer special insights on structuring human societies to exist in balance with the environment. For example, Tibetans are uniquely familiar with life on the Himalayan plateau. This has evolved into a long history of a civilization that took care not to overwhelm and destroy its fragile ecosystem. Tibetans have long appreciated the presence of wild animals as symbolic of freedom. A deep reverence for nature is apparent in much of Tibetan art and ceremony. Spiritual development thrived despite limited material progress. Just as species may not adapt to relatively sudden environmental changes, human cultures also need to be treated with special care to ensure survival. Therefore, learning about the useful ways of people and preserving their cultural heritage is also a part of learning to care for the environment.

"Thinking Globally: A Universal Task"

🌿

Tapping the limited resources of our world—particularly those of the developing nations—simply to fuel consumerism is disastrous. If it continues unchecked, eventually we will all suffer. We must respect the delicate matrix of life and allow it to replenish itself.

—*"Universal Responsibility and Our Global Environment"*

🌿

Since negligence of the environment—which has resulted in lots of harm to the human community—came about by ignorance of the very special importance of the environment, I think it is very important first of all to impart this knowledge within human beings. So it is very important to teach or tell people about its importance for our own benefit.

—*Address, 1996*

🌿

The United Nations Environment Program warns, I'm told, that we are facing the most massive wave of extinction in sixty-five million years. This fact is profoundly frightening. It must open our minds to the immense proportions of the crisis we face. Ignorance of Interdependence has not only harmed the natural environment but human society as well. Instead of caring for one another, we place most of our efforts for happiness in pursuing individual material consumption. We have become so engrossed in this pursuit that, without knowing it, we have neglected to foster the most basic human needs of love, kindness, and cooperation. This is very sad.

—"**Universal Responsibility and Our Global Environment**"

In ancient times, when human ability was limited, we were very aware of the importance of nature, and so we respected nature. Then the time came when we, developed through science and technology, had more ability, and now sometimes it seems people forget about the importance of nature. Sometimes we get some kind of wrong belief that we human beings can control nature with the help of technology. Of course, in certain limited areas we can to a certain extent. But with the globe as a whole it is impossible. Therefore now the time has come to be aware of the importance of nature, the importance of our globe. One day we might find all living things on this planet—including human beings—are extinct.

—**Address, 1992**

Destruction of nature and natural resources results from ignorance, lack of respect for the Earth's living things, and greed. In the first place we must strive to overcome these states of mind by developing an awareness of the interdependent nature of all phenomena, an attitude of wishing not to harm other living creatures, and understanding of the need for compassion. Because of the interdependent nature of everything we cannot hope to solve the multifarious problems with a one-sided or self-centered attitude. History shows us how often in the past people have failed to cooperate. Our failures in the past are a result of ignorance of our interdependent nature.

—*Caring for the Earth*

ᘏ

As people alive today, we must consider future generations: a clean environment is a human right like any other. It is therefore part of our responsibility toward others to ensure that the world we pass on is as healthy, if not healthier, than we found it.

—*Address, 1973*

ᘏ

Modern World

Today, we are truly a global family. What happens in one part of the world may affect us all. This, of course, is not only true of the negative things that happen, but is equally valid for the positive developments. We not only know what happens elsewhere, thanks to the extraordinary modern communications technology, we are also directly affected by events that occur far away. We feel a sense of sadness when children are starving in eastern Africa. Similarly, we feel a sense of joy when a family is reunited after decades of separation by the Berlin Wall. Our crops and livestock are contaminated and our health and livelihood threatened when a nuclear accident happens miles away in another country. Our own security is enhanced when peace breaks out between warring parties in other continents.

—*Nobel Lecture, 1989*

Our world is growing smaller, politically and economically more interdependent, and the world's people are becoming increasingly like one community. Yet we are also being drawn together by the very serious problems we face: overpopulation, dwindling natural resources, and an environmental crisis. In the circumstances we have an obligation to promote a new vision of society, one in which war has no place in resolving disputes among states, communities, or religions, but in which nonviolence is the preeminent value in all human relations.

—*Disarmament, Peace, and Compassion*

We need to think very deeply and hold consultations to come up with some kind of master plan for a better world. Sometimes, perhaps I think it is a little bit idealistic, but I feel our role should be based on the principles of democracy, freedom, and liberty. I think the ultimate goal should be a demilitarized world. I feel very strongly about this. This may appear very far, and we may face many obstacles. But I believe if we keep our determination and effort, we may find some way to achieve this kind of goal. I usually call this "nirvana" or the salvation of humanity.

—**Address, 1991**

Scientific learning and technological progress are essential for improving the quality of life in the modern world. Still more important is the simple practice of getting to know and better appreciate ourselves and our natural surroundings, whether we are children or adults. If we have a true appreciation for others and resist acting out of ignorance, we will take care of the Earth.

—**"Thinking Globally: A Universal Task"**

With the basic understanding of all humans as brothers and sisters, we can appreciate the usefulness of different systems and ideologies that can accommodate different individuals and groups which have different dispositions, different tastes. For certain people under certain conditions, a certain ideology or cultural heritage is more useful. Each person has the right to choose whatever is most suitable. This is the individual's business, on the basis of deep understanding of all other persons as brothers and sisters.

—**Address, 1983**

꙲

I feel optimistic about the future. The rapid changes in our attitude toward the Earth are also a source of hope. As recently as a decade ago, we thoughtlessly devoured the resources of the world, as if there were no end to them. We failed to realize that unchecked consumerism was disastrous for both the environment and social welfare. Now both individuals and governments are seeking a new ecological and economic order.

—"**Universal Responsibility and Our Global Environment**"

꙲

The most difficult problems in the world, which, in large part, emanate from the most developed societies, stem from an overemphasis on the rewards of material progress, one that has placed in jeopardy the very aspects of our common heritage that, in the past, inspired human beings to be honest, altruistic, and spiritually mature. It is clear to me that material development alone cannot replace the old spiritual or humanitarian values that have been responsible for the progress of world civilization as we know it today. We should try, I feel, to strike a balance between material and spiritual growth.

—**Address, 1988**

꙲

Today, spiritual people are voicing their concern about the intermingling of politics with religion, since they fear the violation of ethics by politics and, according to them, thereby contaminating the purity of religion. This line of thought is both selfish and contradictory. All religions exist to serve and help man, and any divorce from politics is to forsake a powerful instrument for social welfare. Religion and politics are a useful combination for the welfare of man when tempered by correct ethical concepts with a minimum of self-interest.

—*Place of Ethics and Morality in Politics*

🌺

Today, we are faced with many global problems such as poverty, overpopulation, and the destruction of the environment. These are problems that we have to address together. No single community or nation can expect to solve them on its own. This indicates how interdependent our world has become.

—"The True Expression of
Nonviolence Is Compassion"

🌺

Children of today are the makers of the future society. If the future of our society is in any way to be meaningful in terms of our being a member of the world community, then they must have a modern education, conducive to a cosmopolitan outlook of life, as well as being familiar enough with their own culture and tradition in order to retain their distinct identity.

—Statement, March 10, 1980

Our beautiful world is facing many crises. . . . It is not a time to pretend something's good.

—Address, 1996

We are going into deep outer space based on developments of modern technology. However, there are many things left to be examined and thought about with respect to the nature of the mind, what the substantial core of the mind is, and so forth. There is much advice, many precepts with respect to this, but the meaning of all these is love and compassion.

—Address, 1984

Today, ethics and moral principles sadly fall in the shadow of self-interest, particularly in the field of political culture. There is a school of thought which warns the moralists to refrain from politics, as politics is devoid of ethics and moral principles. This is a wrong approach, since politics devoid of ethics does not further the benefits to man and his society, and life without morality will make man no better than beasts. The political concept is not "dirty," a common jargon associated with politics today, but the instruments of our political culture have tempered with and distorted the fundamental concepts of fine ideals to further their own selfish ends.

—*The Place of Ethics and Morality in Politics*

Now, you see, if we have such fears—of potential destruction from the atom bomb—we will suffer greatly from them unless we have inner peace. On top of the usual human suffering, we have more fear, more constant threats. So therefore we need more the teachings of kindness and feelings of brotherhood.

—Address, 1987

I believe strongly that the international community has an obligation to morally and politically support the Chinese democracy movement. It has been wise not to isolate China but instead to make efforts to bring her into the mainstream of the world economy. But economic integration alone is not sufficient. China needs human rights, democracy, and the rule of law. These values are the foundation of a free, dynamic, stable, and peaceful society. Such a society would also offer far greater economic freedom, security, and other advantages. Therefore, every effort should be made to bring China also into the mainstream of the world democracy. In the final analysis it is the dedicated and courageous members of the Chinese democracy movement who will lead China into a future of freedom and democracy and no one else. For that reason the Chinese democracy movement must be given every possible assistance, encouragement, and support.

—Commemorating the Anniversary
of Tiananmen, 1995

I have heard a great many complaints about material progress from Westerners, yet, paradoxically, this progress has been the pride of the Western world. I see nothing wrong with material progress per se, provided man is given precedence over his creations. Although materialistic knowledge has contributed enormously to human welfare, it is not capable of creating lasting happiness. In the United States, where technological development is perhaps more advanced than in any other country, there is still a great deal of mental suffering. This is because materialistic knowledge can only provide the type of happiness that is dependent upon physical conditions; it does not provide the happiness that springs from inner development independent of external factors.

—Address, 1985

The world today is engulfed in conflict and sufferings to such an extent that everyone longs for peace and happiness; that longing has unfortunately led them to be carried away by the pursuit of ephemeral pleasure. But there are a few learned people who, dissatisfied by what is ordinarily seen or experienced, think more deeply and search for true happiness. I believe that the search will continue. As we make greater material progress and are able to satisfy our daily needs more fully, man will continue to search for Truth, not being satisfied with material progress alone. Indeed, I am convinced that the search for Truth will grow even keener.

—The Two Truths

꒳

Our generation has arrived at the threshold of a new era in human history: the birth of a global community. Modern communications, trade, and international relations as well as the security and environmental dilemmas we all face make us increasingly interdependent. No one can live in isolation. Thus, whether we like it or not, our vast and diverse human family must finally learn to live together. Individually and collectively we must assume a greater sense of universal responsibility.

—**Address, 1991**

꒳

One of the most encouraging, moving, and hopeful events in the recent Chinese history has been the democracy movement of 1989. The world had a rare opportunity to see the human face and spirit of China. Millions of Chinese brothers and sisters displayed openly and peacefully their yearning for freedom, democracy, and human dignity. Although they had been born and raised under the slogan that "power grows out of the barrels of guns," they embraced nonviolence in a most impressive way, reflecting the values for which the movement stood.

**Commemorating the Anniversary
of Tiananmen, 1995**

꒳

Something that is very striking to my mind is the gap between the rich modern world, the industrialized nations . . . and the southern poor nations. This gap is not only morally wrong, it is practically also. This is also a problem for the future. Even today there are many problems happening because of this gap. I noticed this very clearly in Europe; you see many job seekers from either North Africa or eastern parts of Europe.

—**Address, 1995**

❧

Now already the East-West division is gone; that is very good. Now a Southern and Northern division is there, mainly in economy. The richer nations, sooner or later, will find some problems because of this gap. So we have to find ways and means to reduce this gap. In this field both sides should have genuine discussions in the spirit of our world, rather than my nation or my continent. This is to the mutual interest of our mutual future. If one side adopts a defensive attitude, or another side seeks only to complain and criticize; that is not good.

—**"Universal Responsibility and the Inner Environment"**

❧

All major religions are basically the same in that they emphasize peace of mind and kindness, but it is very important to practice this in our daily lives, not just in a church or a temple.

—**Address, 1983**

❧

I agree with and believe in the communist ideology which seeks the well-being of human beings in general and the

proletariat in particular, and Lenin's policy of the equality of nationalities. Similarly, I was pleased with the discussions I had with Chairman Mao on ideology and the
policy toward nationalities. If that same ideology and
policy were implemented, they would have brought
much admiration and happiness. However, if one is to
make a general comment on the developments during the
past two decades, there has been a lapse in economic and
educational progress, the basis of human happiness.
Moreover, on account of the hardships caused by the un-
bearable disruptions, there has been a loss of trust between the party and the masses, between the officials and
the masses, among the officials themselves, and also the
masses themselves. By deceiving one another through
false assumptions and misrepresentations, there has
been, in reality, a great lapse and delay in achieving the
real goals. Now signs of dissatisfaction are naturally
emerging from all directions, and these are clear indications that the objectives have not been fulfilled.

—Letter to Deng Xiaoping, March 23, 1981

Today, when the world is becoming increasingly interdependent, the dangers of irresponsible behavior have dramatically increased. In ancient times, problems were
mostly family-sized and were solved at the family level.
Unless we realize that now we are part of one big human
family, we cannot hope to bring about peace and happiness. One nation's problems can no longer be solved by
itself because so much depends on the cooperation of

other states. Therefore, it is not only morally wrong but pragmatically unwise for either individuals or nations to pursue their own happiness oblivious to the aspirations of others who surround them.

—Address, 1985

During this century, the twentieth century, humanity learned many different experiences, including some really tragic ones. So now on the basis of our past experience I think we could cultivate, or we should make proper preparation for, a better future, a happier future. For that, I think one important thing is the general attitude that if material progress develops, then all human problems can stop. I think that kind of attitude, I feel, is wrong. Of course, material development is very, very useful, very important. With the help of technology and science, further development and progress will take place. This is very good. But at the same time, since we are human beings, we are not produced by a machine. We are not part of a machine. We have feelings, feelings of pain and pleasure, and there's a connective power. So therefore, the human requirement, all our requirements, cannot be fulfilled by machines alone, or by money alone.

—Address, 1995

As this dramatic century draws to a close, it is clear that the renewed yearning for freedom and democracy sweeping the globe provides an unprecedented opportunity for building a better world. Freedom is the real source of human happiness and creativity. Only when it is allowed to flourish can a genuinely stable international climate exist.

—Address, 1996

❦

In recent years positive changes have taken place in the world as a whole. It is still changing due to many factors, both internal as well as external. I have a deep conviction that things will change. At the same time, this problem is basically a human-created one. In order to solve this problem, the answer must come from humanity itself. Nothing else can be blamed. The answer or solution must come from ourselves. With this feeling, with this conviction, when I look around my own country and other continents, I see more or less a similar situation existing in other parts of the world.

—Address, 1991

❦

Despite the tragedy at the Tiananmen Square on June 4, 1989, the democracy movement has been able to set a process in motion which I consider irreversible. Brute force, no matter how strongly applied, can never subdue the basic human desire for freedom. People do not like to be bullied, cheated, or lied to by either an individual or a system. Such acts are contrary to the essential human spirit. Therefore, even though those who practice deception and use force may achieve short-term success, eventually they will fail. On the other hand, everyone appreciates truth and respect, for it is really in our blood. Truth is the best guarantor and the real foundation for freedom and democracy.

—**Commemorating the Anniversary**
of Tiananmen, 1995

The United States must not underestimate its role in the world today. As Americans you should be proud of your heritage, proud of the values upon which your Constitution is based. Accordingly, you should not shirk from your responsibility to bring those same fundamental rights and freedoms to people living under totalitarian regimes.

—**Address, 1995**

Artificial barriers that have divided nations and peoples have fallen in recent times. With the dismantling of the Berlin Wall the East-West division, which has polarized the whole world for decades, has now come to an end. We are experiencing a time filled with hope and expectations. Yet there still remains a major gulf at the heart of the human family. By this I am referring to the North-South divide. If we are serious in our commitment to the fundamental principles of equality, principles which, I believe, lie at the heart of the concept of human rights, today's economic disparity can no longer be ignored. It is not enough merely to state that all human beings must enjoy equal dignity. This must be translated into action. We have a responsibility to find ways to achieve a more equitable distribution of the world's resources.

—"**Human Rights and Universal Responsibility**"

Today, human society's major problem is human rights. Through highly developed scientific technology we can solve any material human problem, such as poverty, disease, etc., but at the same time, due to this same technology, we create more fear and more desire. For example, today we fear a sudden explosion of atoms in the world. That sort of thing has become a reality.

—**Address, 1988**

As we approach the end of the twentieth century, we find that the world is becoming one community. We are being drawn together by the grave problems of overpopulation, dwindling natural resources, and an environmental crisis that threatens the very foundation of our existence on this planet. Human rights, environmental protection, and great social and economic equality are all interrelated. I believe that to meet the challenges of our times, human beings will have to develop a greater sense of universal responsibility. Each of us must learn to work not just for oneself, one's own family, or one's nation, but for the benefit of all humankind.

—"**Human Rights and Universal Responsibility**"

꙰

Our entire humanity has a responsibility, particularly this nation. Among others, you have economic power, but the most important thing you have is the opportunity to utilize your human creativity. This is something very good. Therefore, I think America has the potential to make this world straight. Certain activities or certain atmospheres are unhealthy and seem to be very crooked. I think in order to make them straight and more honest, with more human feeling, this nation has the real potential and the ability to correct those smaller nations trying to change the world, but the existing pattern may face some immediate consequences which they cannot face. I think this nation is the only superpower.

—**Address, 1991**

꙰

Nowadays, significant events in one part of the world eventually affect the entire planet. Therefore, we have to treat each major local problem as a global concern from the moment it begins.

—**"Universal Responsibility and Our Global Environment"**

꙰

The world is becoming smaller and smaller. Our interdependent nature is now much stronger and clearer. I think a crisis in one part of the world is essentially a global crisis. It is the same with the modern economic situation, and also the new environmental and ecological problems.

These facts and events show us that humanity needs a wider outlook, a holistic view to solve this crisis, including our own Tibetan issue.

—**Address, 1991**

Today only one superpower remains. . . . (Soon) after the collapse of the Soviet communist bloc, when I was returning from Europe to India, there was a high official from an African state on my plane. When we reached Delhi Airport we were together for a few minutes. I expressed to him that recent developments in the world are very hopeful and positive; now there is no more danger of a nuclear holocaust. I expected his response to be equally positive. But instead he raised another possibility. Before there were two superpowers, so the Third World could manage between the two. Now there is only one power, so we have more fear, more anxiety. We are not sure what kind of future lies ahead. I think and feel this is quite unfortunate. The reason is not because of the American system of liberty, democracy, and freedom, but primarily because of U.S. military forces. Perhaps economic power also has some relevance there.

—**"Universal Responsibility and the Inner Environment"**

I believe that during this century we have learned many negative things. As a result, humanity has become more mature. So I have every reason to believe that the next century will be a nicer and friendlier one. I feel a more harmonious world may be achieved.

—**Address, 1991**

As the twentieth century draws to a close, we find that the world has grown smaller. The world's people have become almost one community. Political and military alliances have created large multinational groups; industry and international trade have produced a global economy. Worldwide communications are eliminating ancient barriers of distance, language, and race. We are also being drawn together by the grave problems we face: overpopulation, dwindling natural resources, and an environmental crisis that threatens our air, water, and trees, along with the vast number of beautiful life forms that are the very foundation of existence on this small planet we share. I believe that to meet the challenge of our times, human beings will have to develop a greater sense of universal responsibility.

—**"Universal Responsibility and
Our Global Environment"**

PART THREE

THE OCCUPATION OF TIBET

TIBET BEFORE
THE OCCUPATION

The land of Tibet occupies the high plateau of Central Asia
to the north and west of the towering Himalaya Mountains. Known for its sweeping pasturelands, its sprawling
mountain ranges, and the thinness of its air, Tibet has
been called the Kingdom on the Roof of the World. The
Tibetans call their country *Pö*, meaning "native land,"
but a more colorful term is also used, *Kangchen*, "The
Land of Snows," acknowledging the harsh winters and
the snows which crown the summits of the mountains
even in summer. While there are extremes in geography
and weather, Tibet historically is one of the world's most
culturally unified lands. Central to Tibetan life—influ-
encing virtually every aspect of its existence—is the joyous embrace by its people of Tibetan Buddhism.

Brought to Tibet from India in the seventh century,
Buddhism gradually attracted followers and replaced the
indigenous shamanistic religion called Bön, and was soon
promoted by the local Tibetan rulers, such as the so-called
Chögyel (or Religious King) Trisong Detsen (c. 740–798),
who founded the first Buddhist monastery, recruited Indian translators, and sent young Tibetans to India to

master Buddhist teachings. From this foundation—a Tibetan debt described by the XIV Dalai Lama as that of a disciple to his master—Mahayana Buddhism overcame hardships, including the collapse of central Tibetan authority in the tenth century, to undergo a second great period of dissemination from the eleventh century. Native schools of Buddhism became predominant (eventually four main schools were formed—the Nyingma, Kagyu, Sakya, and Gelukpa, each with their own nuances and traditions), and the Tibetan Buddhist canon was compiled and preserved in copies printed from superbly carved wooden blocks.

Even as Buddhism prospered, however, the region was overtaken in the thirteenth century by a new power in Central Asia which was to have significant ramifications for the future of Tibet. The Mongols under Genghis Khan carved out one of the largest empires in history, and Tibet fell under attack. The most respected religious leader in the country, Sakya Pandita, journeyed in 1249 to the camp of the Mongol khan and nephew of Genghis Khan, Godan. The Mongol ruler was converted swiftly to Buddhism and accepted the Sakya lamas as the spiritual guides of the Mongol khans in return for Mongol protection of the Tibetans. This development marked a Mongol-Tibetan relationship which lasted for centuries and culminated in 1578 with the visit of the prominent religious figure Sönam Gyatso, head of the then preeminent Gelukpa school, to the Mongol chieftain Altan Khan. The lama received from the chief the honorific title *Ta le*, meaning Ocean, denoting the depths of the lama's boundless wisdom. This title came to be called Dalai Lama, or

Ocean of Wisdom, and was the foundation of the office which has endured into modern times.

Sönam Gyatso was proclaimed the third Dalai Lama, with his two venerated predecessors—the first two heads of the Gelukpa school who brought it to spiritual supremacy in Tibet—termed the first and second Dalai Lamas. The most important of the early Dalai Lamas was the fifth, Ngawang Losang Gyatso (1617–1682), called the Great Fifth. Aside from being a prolific writer and teacher, he was a capable statesman. Through his political acumen Tibet was unified for the first time since the ninth century, and the Dalai Lamas assumed both the temporal and spiritual governance over the country which became a hallmark of Tibetan culture. Even more significant was the V Dalai Lama's emphasis on the Tibetan Buddhist teaching that the incarnation of Chenrezig, the Buddha of compassion (called Avalokiteshvara in the Indian), appeared throughout Tibetan history until manifesting itself in the persons of each of the Dalai Lamas. To give full expression to this doctrine, the V Dalai Lama built the famed Potala Palace to serve as his residence. The name was chosen deliberately to associate the home of the Dalai Lama with the mountain in southern India of the god Siva, in his form as Lokésvara, the Lord of the World, and honored by Tibetans as an emanation of Avalokiteshvara.

In the centuries that followed the death of the Great Fifth, Tibet grew increasingly isolated, its domestic affairs marred by interventions by the Manchus, Mongols, and the Nepalese, and intermittent interference by China. Within the confines of its mountainous borders, the Tibetans fostered perhaps the world's most pure Buddhist culture. Economic development was minimal, partly because of the harshness of the terrain and the difficulties of organizing transportation and industry, but also through the Buddhist traditions of living in close harmony with nature and of respecting all life, even that of animals and plants. Tibet was one of the world's first nations to discourage the wanton consumption of natural resources and to establish provisions for environmental and wildlife protection. In 1642 the V Dalai Lama promulgated a decree for protecting animals and the environment, a law which was reissued annually right up to the communist takeover of the kingdom.

Prior to the invasion of the country by China in 1950, Tibet was far from a perfect paradise, but its people were generally content within their feudal system and were devoted body and mind to their Buddhist life. The depth of their religious faith was visible in the thousands of monasteries which dotted the countryside, the prayer flags which flew over virtually every home, the vast membership in the religious orders, and the faithful way in which the Tibetans followed the calendar of festivals and holy days. Above all, the heart of the nation was the love and veneration given to the Dalai Lamas as both temporal rulers of Tibet and as living deities of compassion.

THE OCCUPATION OF TIBET

The history of modern Tibet was changed forever by the victory of the Chinese Communists over the Chinese

Nationalists (the Kuomintang) and the creation in 1949 of the so-called People's Republic of China. As part of the Communist agenda of bringing the whole of what it claimed to be the Chinese Motherland under one government, Radio Beijing declared that the People's Liberation Army would reacquire all Chinese territories, including Tibet and Taiwan. The following year, on October 7, 1950, the People's Liberation Army carried out its threat. Forty thousand Chinese troops stormed across the frontier, routing the tiny and ill-equipped Tibetan army.

In an emergency session of the Tibetan National Assembly in November, the representatives asked the Dalai Lama—who was only sixteen at the time—to assume full authority over the government. Soon after, the Tibetan Foreign Office sent out an urgent message to the United Nations: *"Tibet recognizes that it is in no position to resist the Chinese advance. . . . Though there is little hope that a nation dedicated to peace will be able to resist the brutal effort of men trained to war, we understand that the U.N. has decided to stop aggression wherever it takes place."*

To give the illusion of legitimacy to the takeover, Beijing had compelled a delegation of Tibetan representatives to sign a seventeen-point treaty called Measures for the Peaceful Liberation of Tibet on May 23, 1951, forging the Tibetan seals which were affixed to the document. By its terms Tibet's external affairs were subject to Chinese authority, while Beijing guaranteed regional autonomy, full religious rights, and the power of both the Panchen and the Dalai Lamas.

On September 9, 1951, the first elements of the People's Liberation Army marched into Lhasa. For the first time in its long history, Tibet was under the direct control of China. The communist occupation forces proclaimed the county to be liberated from its feudal overlords and launched a massive propaganda effort, with promises of extensive modernization, schools, hospitals, railroads, and cinemas. Chinese radio, newspapers, public pronouncements, and films assailed the government of the Dalai Lama, belittled all aspects of Tibetan Buddhism, and called traditional Tibetan culture backward. Initially patient with the hostile Tibetan response, the Chinese were soon driven to exasperation by the tiny number of collaborators and the absolute unwillingness of the mass of Tibetans to embrace communism.

Accepting that propaganda had failed, the Chinese turned to intimidation and force. One of the most common methods was to arrest respected religious and government leaders, charge them with crimes against the people, and subject them to brutal mock trials, which included abuse, torture, and finally execution. Unable to bear the cruel treatment of its monks, nuns, and helpless civilians, the Tibetans rose up in sporadic revolts, an unprecedented event for the country. Thousands of Tibetans were arrested and executed in reprisals, and the agrarian reforms—meaning the seizure of land and liquidation of the country's landowners—were accelerated, thereby aggravating Tibetan guerrilla activities.

Despite the efforts to negotiate with the Chinese and his incessant pleas for nonviolence, the Dalai Lama sensed the coming of tragedy. Tensions in Lhasa and elsewhere in the country reached a crisis point in March 1959 with the apparent Chinese plan to seize the Dalai Lama at a theatrical performance to which he had been invited by the Chinese military, with the stipulation that he come alone and without bodyguards. Crowds of angry Tibetans gathered at the Norbulingka Palace to protect the Dalai Lama. They were soon joined by tens of thousands of protesters chanting anti-Chinese slogans. Other mass gatherings were staged throughout Lhasa. The Chinese response was to shell the crowds at the Norbulingka. Within days of the March 10, 1959, uprising nearly fifteen thousand Tibetans had been killed, their bodies literally strewn through the streets of Lhasa. Facing death or capture by the Chinese and recognizing the futility of negotiations, the Dalai Lama fled to India. Eighty thousand Tibetans followed him into exile. On March 28, Chinese premier Zhou Enlai declared the government of Tibet to be dissolved.

Ending all pretense of benign overlordship, the Chinese army unleashed its full fury upon Tibet. In little over a year, some 87,000 Tibetans were dead in central Tibet. Both the Potala and the Norbulingka were shelled, the two sacred sites of Ganden Monastery and Ramoche Temple were destroyed, and martial law was declared.

Central to the Chinese effort to subjugate Tibet was its relentless war on religion. Declaring that communism and religion were two forces that could not coexist, the Chinese occupation forces focused most of their oppression on the monastic orders, the monastic schools, temples, and shrines, and the simple faith of the Tibetan people. By 1976, only a handful of Tibet's 6,259 monasteries and convents were left standing. Over a quarter of a million monks and nuns were forced to give up their religious life, and over one hundred thousand had been tortured, abused, and murdered. Sacred and ancient texts were burned or placed in military latrines. The sacred temples were plundered of their gold, precious gems, and other metals before being dynamited. Thousands of irreplaceable vessels, statues, paintings, and artifacts were trucked away to China. These were either melted down for their precious metals or sold on the international market as antiques to raise foreign currency.

To handle the thousands of detainees and to provide a pool for labor in the initial reconstruction programs, the Chinese established a series of prison and labor camps. Those consigned to prison camps—such as older monks—faced torture, execution, starvation, and disease, while prisoners in the labor camps served as slave workers for the systematic exploitation of Tibet's natural resources.

As terrible as the situation was in the wake of the suppressed uprising of 1959, conditions became even more severe from 1966, when Tibet was subjected to the full brunt of the Cultural Revolution, the immense reordering of Chinese society along the most radical lines of communist ideology. Units of fanatical Red Guards perpetrated a decade-long reign of terror during which thousands were murdered and rape gangs stalked the countryside to sow fear in the population.

With the death of Mao Zedong in 1976, the Cultural Revolution was brought to a close, and Deng Xiaoping initiated what proved to be a marked movement by China toward economic liberalization. Deng admitted that "mistakes were made" in Tibet; martial law was lifted and a widely trumpeted liberalization program commenced in Tibet. The Chinese were most anxious to promote a new policy of granting apparent religious freedom. A small portion of monastic buildings were rebuilt, schools were reopened, and many of the outward ritual practices of Buddhism were permitted, such as the use of prayer flags, incense, and public worship.

International human rights organizations have documented that the religious reforms have done little to reverse China's campaign against Buddhism and all religion in Tibet. Severe limitations are in place on the curricula of the monastic colleges, with only approved students (those who have studied Marxism, are sympathetic to the Communist Party, and who have denounced the Dalai Lama) gaining admission. Textbooks, instructors, and supplies are desperately needed. The legitimate Buddhist rites are conducted usually only for tourists, and the monks are under constant surveillance by spies and informers, and are subject to arrest and torture for the slightest transgressions. The Dalai Lama noted the superficiality of these changes in his Statement of March 10, 1984, on the twenty-fifth anniversary of the Tibetan uprising:

> Although much publicity has been made about the freedom of religious worship by restoring a few of the destroyed monasteries, obstructions are still placed on those entering the monastic order and those who start to preach, study, and practice the Dharma. . . . The so-called freedom of religious worship and nationalities' autonomy, though impressive slogans, are simply empty talk.

Just as the religious reforms proved illusory, so too did the economic liberalization of China fail to engender any meaningful improvement in human rights. Political freedom never materialized in Tibet, and throughout the 1980s political activists and protesters were arrested, imprisoned, and tortured. Police crackdowns consistently failed to quell dissent, however. Demonstrations across Tibet were common, met with extreme force by Chinese security forces. In 1988 the Beijing regime announced a crackdown on all forms of dissent, an operation which climaxed with the declaration on March 7, 1989, of martial law across Lhasa. Hundreds were killed and thousands more arrested in what proved to be a Tibetan prelude to the Tiananmen Square massacre inflicted upon the Chinese people by the Beijing regime later that year.

Martial law was lifted in May 1990, but security forces in Tibet retained broad powers to arrest, detain, and torture anyone suspected of dissent or activities against Chinese rule. In 1992 the Chinese embarked upon a new wave of house-to-house searches for all materials considered subversive. These ranged from Buddhist books to anything related to the Dalai Lama, including his speeches, tapes, prayers, and books. Three years later an official ban was once more declared against all images of the Dalai Lama, a prohibition which had been in place for many years and which had been lifted only in 1979.

TIBET TODAY

Tibetans today live under one of the most restrictive police states anywhere on the planet. They may be arrested and imprisoned without trial for offenses ranging from speaking to foreigners, possessing photographs or writings of the Dalai Lama, singing traditional Tibetan songs, or speaking publicly about the Chinese occupation. All forms of assembly outside of approved pro-Chinese rallies or orchestrated events are prohibited and result in violent countermeasures by the organs of Chinese security.

Movement or travel by Tibetans is curtailed severely, in direct violation of Article 13 of the Universal Declaration of Human Rights. It is forbidden to journey from one town to another without official permission. All Tibetans must be registered in their places of residence, but at a moment's notice they can be expelled from their homes and forced to move to any location designated by Chinese officials.

Tibetans who are detained for the crimes usually classified as "illegal separatist activity" are subject to automatic torture, incarceration without any due process, and execution without any appeal. In many cases, families are not informed of arrests or executions, their missing relatives literally disappearing in the night. A recent example of this judicial system was the trial of Tibetan refugee and Fulbright scholar Ngawang Choephel, who was sentenced by a court in Shigatse to eighteen years in prison for being a "spy" for the "Dalai clique." No details at all were forthcoming from China beyond its announcement on December 26, 1996, on Lhasa Radio. United States Senator Daniel P. Moynihan observed that Choephel's sentence was "indicative of the extreme measures the Chinese government continues to take to repress all forms of Tibetan cultural expression."

The human rights condition in Tibet has been documented extensively by numerous international organizations, including Amnesty International and Asia Watch. Their findings have been corroborated by many independent fact-finding committees from around the world, including India, Australia, Austria, and Switzerland. In 1985 the U.N. Commission on Human Rights received appeals from various organizations to seek some solution to the pervasive violations of basic rights in Tibet by the Chinese. As the evidence mounted, resolutions were passed by the legislative bodies of West Germany (1987), Italy (1989), Australia (1990), the European Parliament (1987, 1989, and 1990), and both the U.S. Senate and House of Representatives demanding that China respect the rights of the Tibetan people. Assorted U.N. committees have also expressed their anxiety, such as the Committee Against Torture and the Committee on the Elimination of All Forms of Racial Discrimination.

Beyond the constant threat of arrest, Tibetans in their own country face discrimination in educational, medical, economic, and political opportunities, and are being marginalized through a policy of state-sponsored Chinese immigration into Tibet. The sinicization of Tibet, the better health care and education, and the open favor shown to Chinese immigrants is not a coincidental policy, but is part of a deliberate and far-reaching program which seeks the eradication of Tibetan culture. As the Dalai Lama said in 1991: *"Tibet is being colonized by waves of Chinese immigrants. We are becoming a minority in our own country. The new Chinese settlers have created an alternate society: a Chinese apartheid which, denying Tibetans equal social and economic status in our own land, threatens to finally overwhelm and absorb us.''*

Four years later the Dalai Lama lamented: *''China has encouraged millions of Chinese to settle in Tibet in order to eliminate all vestiges of Tibet as a land for Tibetans. This is China's idea of a 'final solution' to its Tibet problem. Already today Tibetans are marginalized in many major towns and cities. If this population transfer is allowed to continue, Tibetan civilization will cease to exist.''*

Through a policy of population transfer, forced immigration of Chinese workers, and the stationing of around five hundred thousand troops across Tibet, China has succeeded in planting a majority population on the foreign soil of Tibet. The Tibetan population in 1959 was approximately six million, spread out across the three traditional provinces of Amdo, Kham, and U-Tsang. By the early 1980s, it was estimated that there were over seven and a half million Chinese in Tibet. When figured with deaths of over a million Tibetans between 1959 and the 1980s, the permanent exile of another one hundred fifty thousand, and the imprisonment of untold thousands of others, the Chinese now possess a clear majority in the occupied country.

According to documents released by the Chinese government itself in 1985, it was the intention of the People's Republic to continue the migration into Tibet to such a degree that by the second decade of the next century, there would be as many as sixty million Chinese in Tibet. Not only has this policy continued, recent reports point to its expansion. The effect of this migration signals the irreversible demolition of Tibetan culture, realizing the ambition of Beijing to make the Tibetan plateau and the Land of Snows truly a Chinese domain.

The Chinese dominance is seen in the prevalence of the Chinese language. In 1966 the occupation government forbade the teaching of Tibetan, and all teachers in schools were required to conduct their courses in Chinese. Official government documents are published in Chinese; streets, buildings, roads, and the bulk of geographical locations have been renamed in Chinese. Those Tibetans serving in the government today rarely speak Tibetan and so are incapable of communicating with the majority of Tibetans, who have not learned Chinese or whose knowledge of it is limited owing to poor educational facilities.

The Chinese population influx has a decidedly practical purpose as well as cultural and political ones: total exploitation of Tibet's vast storehouse of natural resources. From the time of the full seizure of Tibet, China has stripped Tibet of its minerals, forests, and wildlife. The pillaging of the Tibetan environment marks a complete reversal of the region's history of protecting its natural resources and has brought an environmental crisis that threatens the ecological and meteorological balance of Central Asia.

Over 68 percent of the ancient forests of Tibet have been cut down, the wood shipped off to China for use in industry and construction. As the typical method of deforestation is clear cutting, reforestation is nearly impossible because of Tibet's demanding and extreme weather and the rapid processes of soil degradation and erosion of the once thriving slopes of the lower Himalayas. With deforestation so extensive, desertification has wide ramifications for India and elsewhere, where flooding has increased and where there has been a disruption in recent decades of traditional weather patterns.

Adding to the erosion is the pillage of mineral deposits through strip mining and indiscriminate mining for plutonium, oil, coal, gold, shale, iron, lead, and copper with no concern for environmental safeguards. Tibet now suffers from heavy chemical pollution, especially in its rural areas, where deformities and serious birth defects have been reported by Tibetan human rights organizations.

With mining has also come the utilization of the Tibetan plateau as a staging point for nuclear weapons and nuclear and toxic waste. As China pushes its strategic interests ever westward toward India, Turkestan, Pakistan, and the Near East, Beijing has stationed a quarter of its nuclear arsenal in Tibet, along with nuclear weapons research facilities. This is in total contradiction to Buddhist teachings and a personally troubling development for the Dalai Lama, who advocates global nuclear disarmament. The facilities for nuclear research produce waste which has been treated in much the same way as the mining waste. Pollutants are today found in the soil, air, and especially the intricate network of Tibet's rivers, which carry water into a host of neighboring countries.

Beyond the toll on human communities, one effect of China's exploitation is the swift eradication of Tibetan wildlife. Currently, there are over thirty species in Tibet on endangered-animal lists. Recent years have brought the slaughter of Tibet's herds of wild yaks and asses and the sharp decline of such species as the Tibetan white-lipped deer, Tibetan snow leopard, and wild blue Tibetan sheep.

No episode in modern Tibetan history has been more emblematic of the Chinese occupation than that of the Panchen Lama. The second most important spiritual leader in Tibet behind the Dalai Lama—the lama traditionally heads the influential Tashilhunpo monastery—the post is, like that of the Dalai Lama, one filled through the search for the reincarnation of the deceased predecessor. In 1995, shortly after the Dalai Lama recognized six-year-old Gandun Chokyi Nyima as the reincarnated Panchen Lama, Chinese security forces kidnapped the boy and his family. Appeals from the Dalai Lama and a resolution from the European Parliament were ignored, and the Tibetan government-in-exile knows only that the *tülku* (the reincarnated lama) has been moved to China and is still alive. Soon after the kidnapping, Chinese authorities announced the discovery of their own "recognized reincarnation" of the Panchen Lama. By coincidence, the child was the son of two members of the Tibetan Communist Party.

Appendix One

THE DALAI LAMA'S ACCEPTANCE SPEECH OF THE 1989 NOBEL PEACE PRIZE

I am deeply touched to be chosen as this year's recipient of the Nobel Peace Prize. I believe my selection reaffirms the universal values of nonviolence, peace, and understanding between all members of our great human family. We all desire a happier, more humane, and harmonious world, and I have always felt that the practice of love and compassion, tolerance and respect for others, is the most effective manner in which to bring this about. I hope this prize will provide courage to the six million people of Tibet. For some forty years now Tibetans have been undergoing the most painful period of our long history. During this time over a million of our people have perished, and more than six thousand monasteries—the seat of our peaceful culture—have been destroyed. There is not a single family, either in Tibet or among the refugees abroad, which has gone unscathed.

Yet our people's determination and commitment to spiritual values and the practice of nonviolence remain unshaken. This prize is a profound recognition of their faith and perseverance.

The demonstrations which have rocked Tibet for the

past two years continue to be nonviolent despite the brutal suppression. Since the imposition of martial law in
Lhasa last March, Tibet has been sealed off, and while
global attention has focused on the tragic events in China,
a systematic effort to crush the spirit and national identity of the Tibetan people is being pursued by the government of the People's Republic.

Tibetans today are facing the real possibility of elimination as a people and as a nation. The government of the
People's Republic of China is practicing a form of genocide
by relocating millions of Chinese settlers into Tibet. I ask
that this massive population transfer be stopped. Unless
the cruel and inhuman treatment of my people is brought
to an end and until they are given their due right to self-
determination, there will always be obstacles in finding a
solution to the Tibetan issue.

I accept the Nobel Peace Prize in a spirit of optimism
despite the many grave problems which humanity faces
today. We all know the immensity of the challenges facing our generation: the problem of overpopulation, the
threat to our environment, and the dangers of military
confrontation. As this dramatic century draws to a close,
it is clear that the renewed yearning for freedom and democracy sweeping the globe provides an unprecedented
opportunity for building a better world. Freedom is the
real source of human happiness and creativity. Only
when it is allowed to flourish can a genuinely stable international climate exist. The suppression of the rights and
freedoms of any people by totalitarian governments is
against human nature, and the recent movement for democracy in various parts of the world is a clear indication
of this.

The Chinese students have given me great hope for the future of China and Tibet. I feel that their movement follows the tradition of Mahatma Gandhi's *ahimsa* or nonviolence, which has deeply inspired me since I was a small boy. The eventual success of all people seeking a more tolerant atmosphere must derive from a commitment to counter hatred and violence with patience. We must seek change through dialogue and trust. It is my heartfelt prayer that Tibet's plight may be resolved in such a manner and that once again my country, the roof of the world, may serve as a sanctuary of people and as a resource of spiritual inspiration at the heart of Asia. I hope and pray that the decision to give me the Nobel Peace Prize will encourage all those who pursue the path of peace to do so in a renewed spirit of optimism and strength.

Appendix Two

BOOKS AUTHORED BY HIS HOLINESS THE XIV DALAI LAMA

Beyond Dogma: Dialogues and Discourses, trans. by Alison Anderson, 1996.

The World of Tibetan Buddhism, ed. by Geshe Thupten Jinpa, 1995.

The Power of Compassion, 1995.

The Way to Freedom, trans. by Donald Lopez, 1995.

Awakening the Mind, Lightening the Heart, trans. by Donald Lopez, 1995.

The Path to Enlightenment, trans. & ed. by Glenn H. Mullin, 1995.

Essential Teachings, 1995.

Violence & Compassion: Power of Buddhism, with Jean-Claude Carriäre, 1995.

Dialogues on Universal Responsibility & Education, 1995.

A Flash of Lightning in the Dark of Night, 1994.

The Meaning of Life from a Buddhist Perspective, trans. by Jeffrey Hopkins, 1992.

Freedom in Exile: The Autobiography of the Dalai Lama, 1991.

My Tibet, with Galen Rowell, 1991.

Path to Bliss, ed. by Thupten Jinpa & Christine Cox, 1991.

The Global Community and the Need for Universal Responsibility, 1991.

Compassion and the Individual, 1991.

Cultivating a Daily Meditation, 1991.

The Dalai Lama: A Policy of Kindness, ed. by Sidney Piburn, 1990.

The Dalai Lama at Harvard: Lectures on the Buddhist Path to Peace, trans. by Jeffrey Hopkins, 1989.

The Bodhgaya Interviews, 1981–85, ed. by Jose Ignacio Cabezon, 1988.

Commentary on Shantideva—Transcendent Wisdom, trans. and annotated by B. Alan Wallace, 1988.

The Union of Bliss and Emptiness, 1988.

A Long Look Homeward: An Interview with the Dalai Lama of Tibet, with Glenn H. Mullin, 1987.

Kalachakra: Rite of Initiation, 1985.

Opening the Eye of New Awareness, trans. by Donald S. Lopez, Jr., with Jeffrey Hopkins, 1985.

Kindness, Clarity, and Insight, trans. and ed. by Jeffrey Hopkins, co-ed. by Elizabeth Napper, 1984.

A Human Approach to World Peace, 1984.

Advice from Buddha Shakyamuni, trans. by Jeremy Russell and Tsepak Rigzin, 1982.

Four Essential Buddhist Commentaries, 1982.

Deity Yoga, trans. and ed. by Tsong-ka-pa and Jeffrey Hopkins, 1981.

An Interview with the Dalai Lama, with John F. Avedon, 1980.

Tantra in Tibet, trans. and ed. by Tsong-ka-pa and Jeffrey Hopkins, 1977.

Universal Responsibility and the Good Heart, 1977.

The Buddhism of Tibet, trans. & ed. by Jeffrey Hopkins, 1975.

The Buddhism of Tibet and the Key to the Middle Way, 1975.

The Opening of the Wisdom Eye, 1972.

Happiness, Karma and Mind, 1969.

An Introduction to Buddhism, 1965.

My Land and My People, 1964.

A Tantric Meditation, n.d.

The Eight Verses of Training the Mind, n.d.

Aryasura's Aspiration & A Meditation on Compassion, n.d.

Appendix Three

TIBETAN SUPPORT ORGANIZATIONS

The following is a list of current organizations working to bring about Tibetan independence or to aid the many Tibetans in chronic need of medical assistance, both in Tibet and in exile around the globe. Readers are encouraged to assist these organizations.

- The Office of Tibet
  241 E. 32nd St.
  New York, NY 10016
  Tel: (212) 213-5010
  Fax: 212-779-9245
  E-mail: otny@igc.apc.org

  The main office of the Tibetan government-in-exile for North America.

- The Office of Tibet
  Tibet House
  1 Culworth St.
  London NW8 7AF, U.K.
  Tel: (44-171) 722 5378
  Fax: (44-171) 722-0362

  The main office of the Tibetan government-in-exile in the United Kingdom.

- The Office of Tibet
  3 Weld St.
  Yarralumla
  Canberra ACT, 2600
  Tel: (61-6) 285-4046

  The main office of the Tibetan government-in-exile in Australia.

- International Campaign for Tibet
  1735 Eye St. N.W.
  Suite 615
  Washington, D.C. 20006
  Tel: (202) 785-1515
  Fax: (202) 785-4343
  E-mail: ict@igc.apc.org

- Committee of 100 for Tibet
  P.O. Box 60612
  Palo Alto, CA 94306
  Tel/Fax: (415) 851-4262
  E-mail: Tibet100@aol.com

  A prestigious organization that includes among its members Elie Wiesel, Coretta Scott King, John Cleese, Theodore Hesburgh, and Richard Gere. It publishes a monthly *Tibet News Digest*.

- Tibet House
  241 E. 32nd St.
  New York, NY 10016
  Tel: (212) 213-5592
  Fax: (212) 213-6408

  An organization established by actor Richard Gere to preserve Tibet's cultural heritage.

- Students for a Free Tibet
  241 E. 32nd St.
  New York, NY 10016
  Tel: (212) 213-5011
  Fax: (212) 779-9245
  E-mail: ustcsft@igc.apc.org

  A major organization devoted to organizing student
  awareness about Tibet and to work for placing political pressure to change current policies concerning
  the Tibetan question.

- U.S. Tibet Committee
  241 E. 32nd St.
  New York, NY 10016

  A human rights organization devoted to document-
  ing conditions in Tibet.

- Tibetan Women's Association
  P.O. Box 31966
  Seattle, WA 98210-3066
  Fax: (206) 547-3758
  E-mail: trcseattle@igc.apc.org

- Tibetan Nuns Project
  P.O. Box 374
  San Geronimo, CA 94963
  Tel: (415) 488-1325

- Free Tibet Campaign
  1 Rosoman Place
  London EC1R 0JY
  Tel: (44-171) 833-9958
  Fax: (44-171) 833-3838

- Tibet Information Network
  City Cloisters
  188-196 Old St.
  London EC1V 9FR
  Tel: (44-171) 814-9011
  Fax: (44-171) 814-9015
  E-mail: tin@tibetinfo.net

- Los Angeles Friends of Tibet
  P.O. Box 641066
  Los Angeles, CA 90064
  Tel: (310) 289-4653
  E-mail: friendstibet@igc.apc.org

- The Tibetan Nyingma Relief Foundation
  2425 Hillside Ave.
  Berkeley, CA 94704
  Tel: (510) 845-1710

- Milarepa Fund
  76 Uranus Terrace
  San Francisco, CA 94114

- The Norbulingka Institute
  c/o Johnny Whitright
  P.O. Dishpur 176057
  Dharamsala
  HP India
  Tel: 91-1892-24982
  Fax: 91-1892-22010

- The Tibetan Refugee Health Care Project
  Dr. Marsha Woolf, Director
  P.O. Box 2116
  Providence, RI 02905

- Canadian Tibet Committee
  4675 Coolbrook
  Montreal, Quebec
  Canada H3X 2K7
  Tel: (514) 487-0665
  Fax: (514) 487-7825
  E-mail: fourniel@ERE.UMontreal.CA

- International Committee of Lawyers for Tibet
  2288 Fulton St.
  Suite 312
  Berkeley, CA 94704
  Tel: (510) 486-0588
  Fax: (510) 548-3785
  E-mail: iclt@igc.apc.org

- U.S. Tibetan Society for School and Culture
  c/o Anne Oliver
  4707 Connecticut Ave. N.W. #201
  Washington, D.C. 20008

- Bay Area Friends of Tibet
  2288 Fulton St.
  Suite 312
  Berkeley, CA 94704
  Tel: (510) 548-1271
  E-mail: bafot@igc.apc.org